fishing mates

Peter Slater

FOR THE LOVE OF

fishing and mates

mate1
/meɪt/
noun
suffix: -mates; plural noun: mates
1.
the sexual partner of a bird or other animal.
"a male bird sings to court a mate"
2.
a fellow member or joint occupant of a specified thing.
"his table-mates"

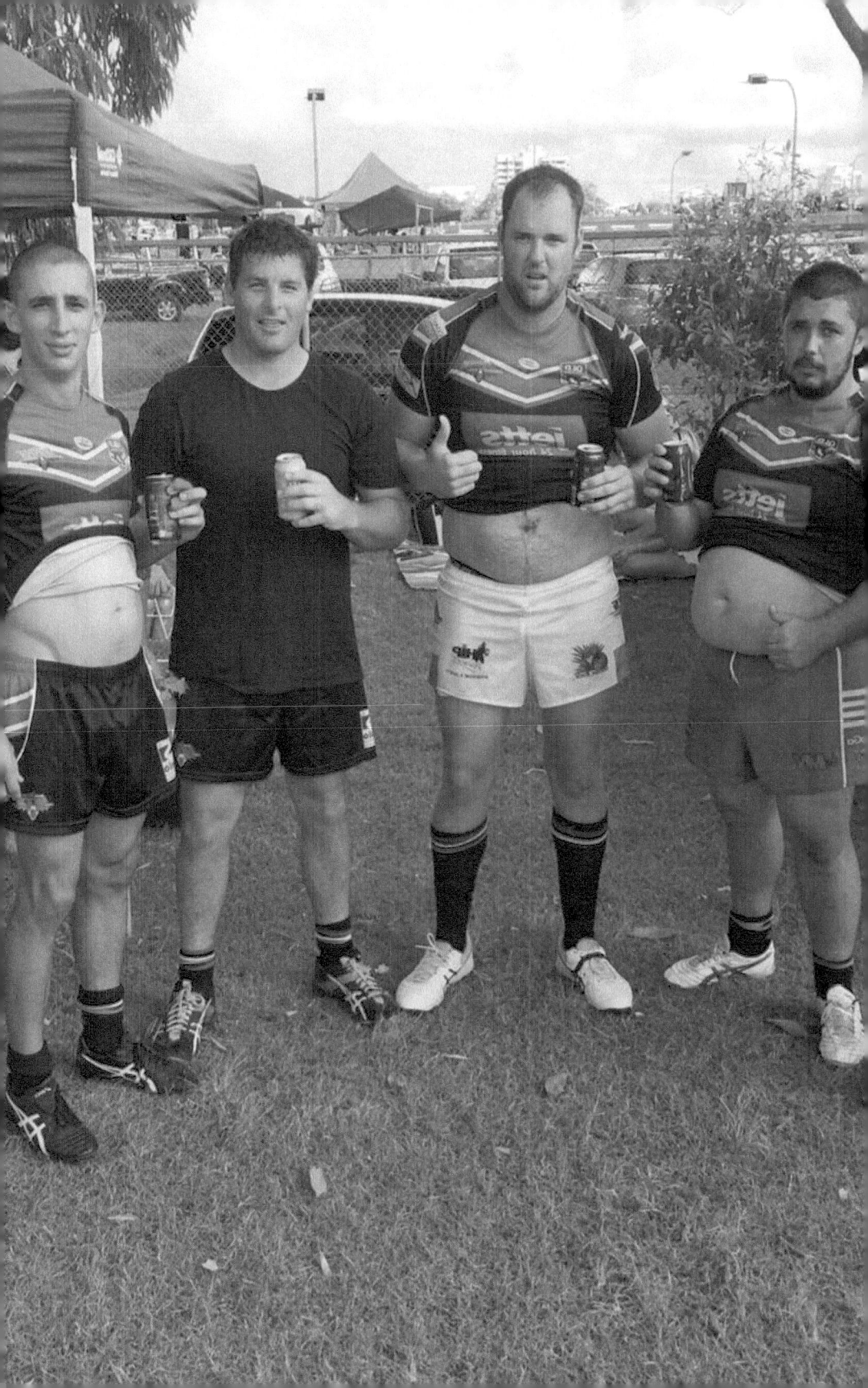

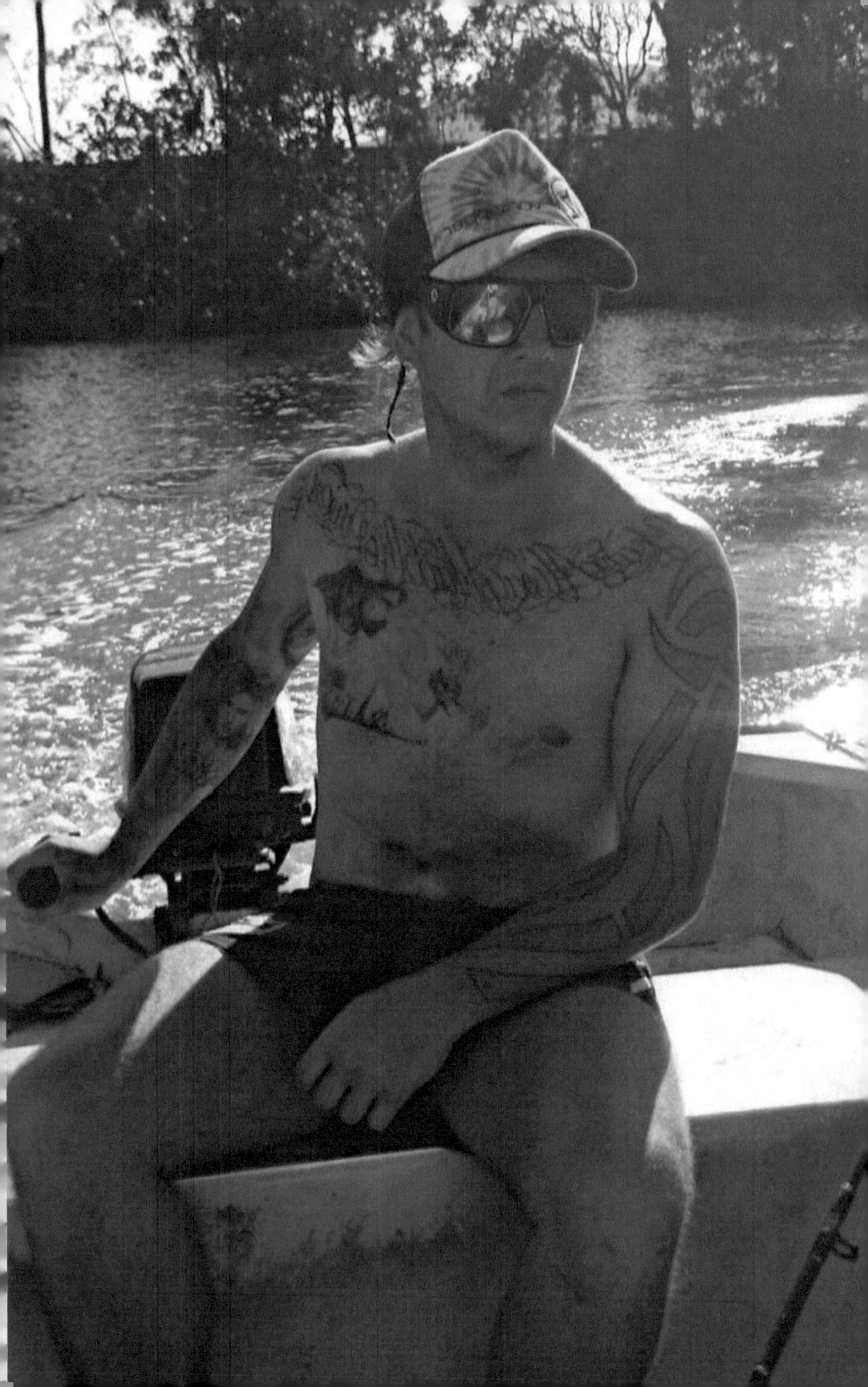

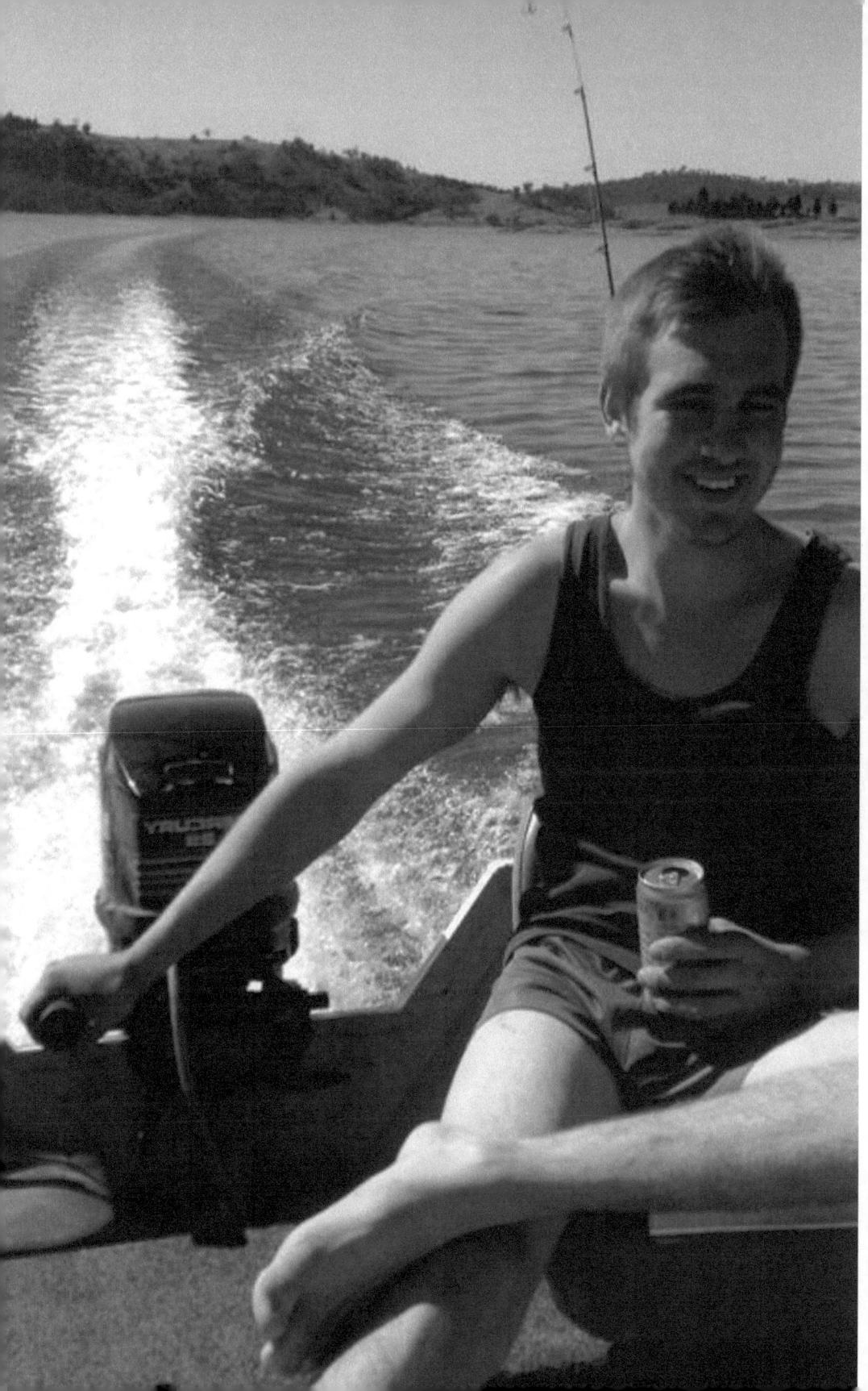

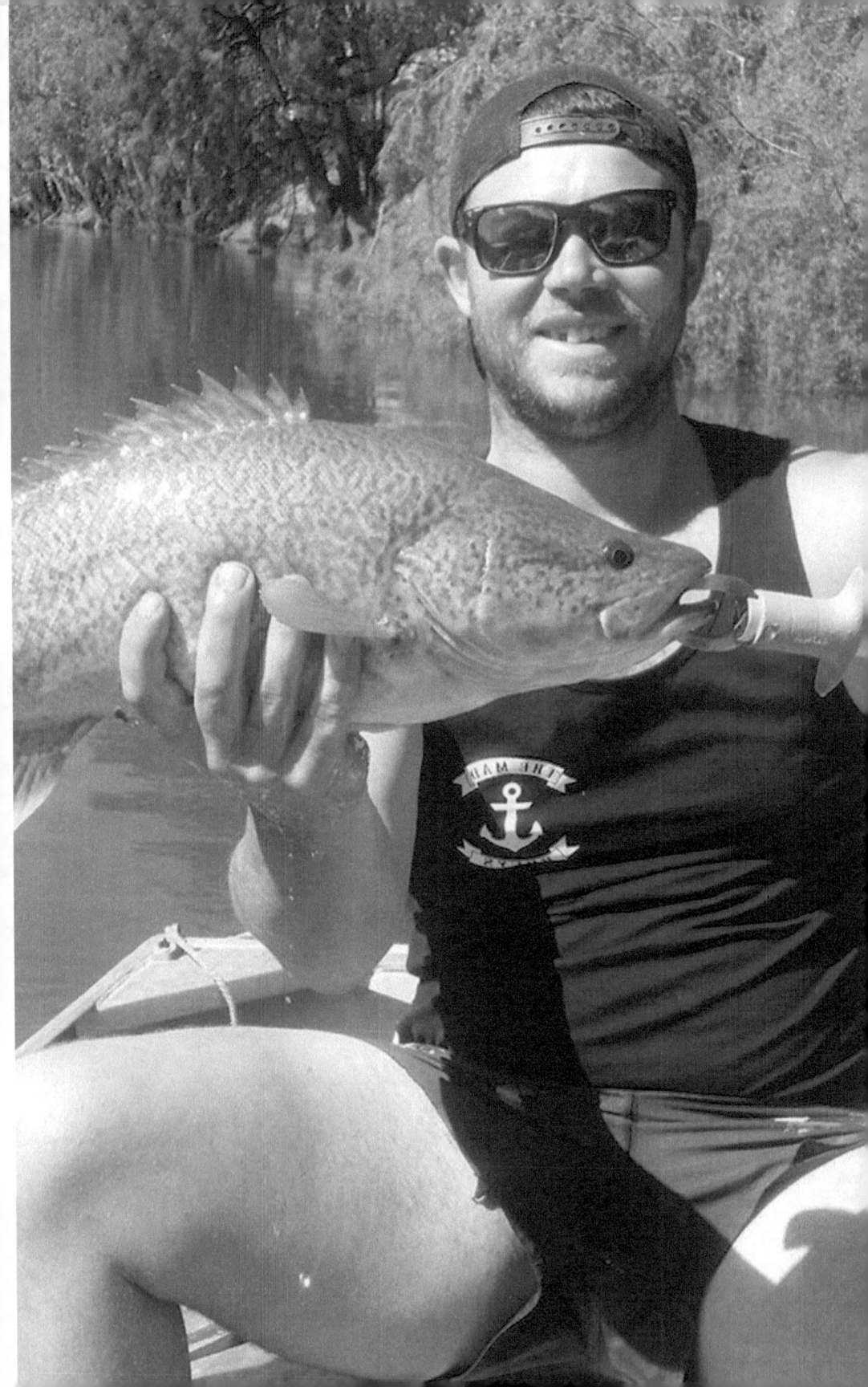

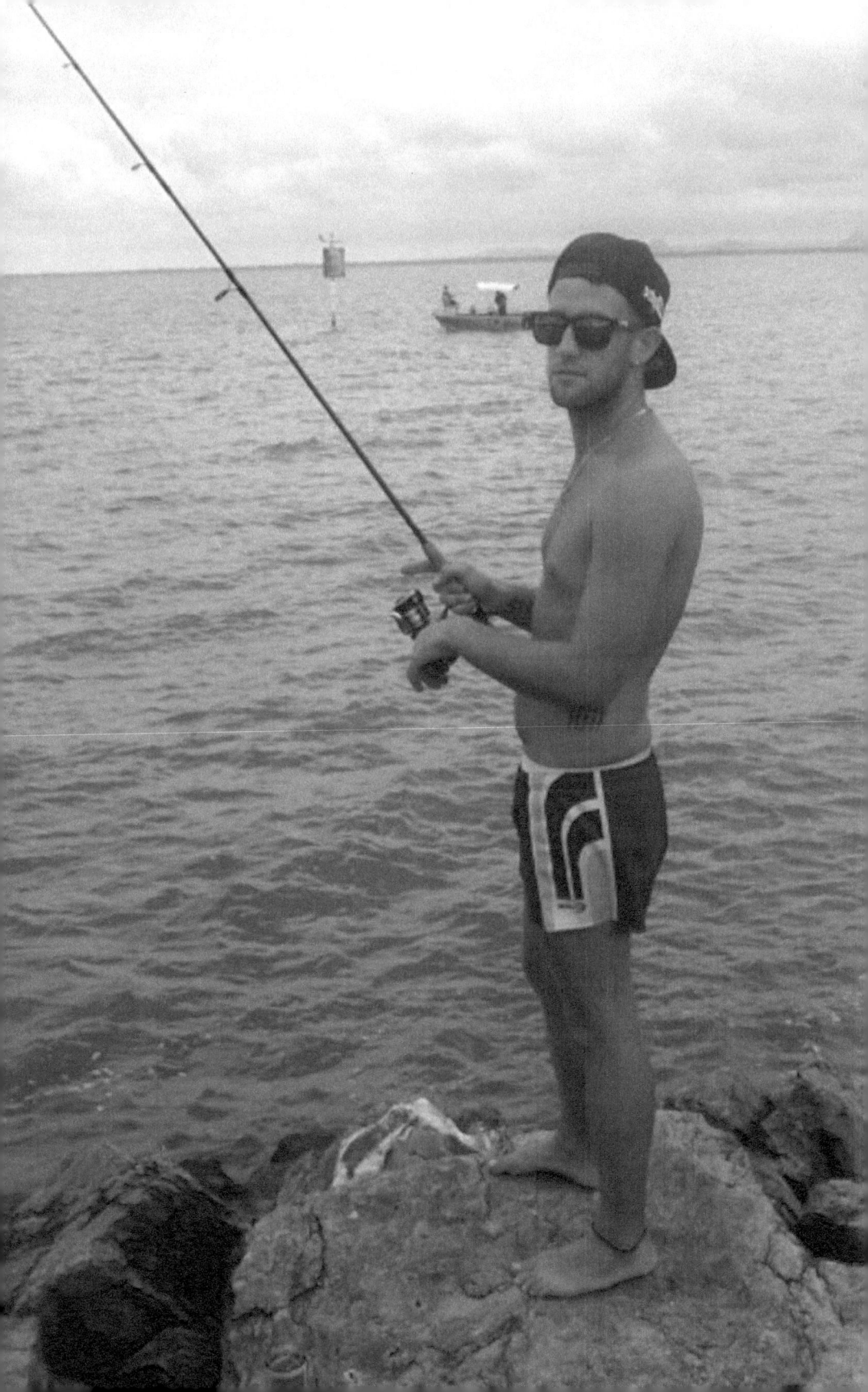

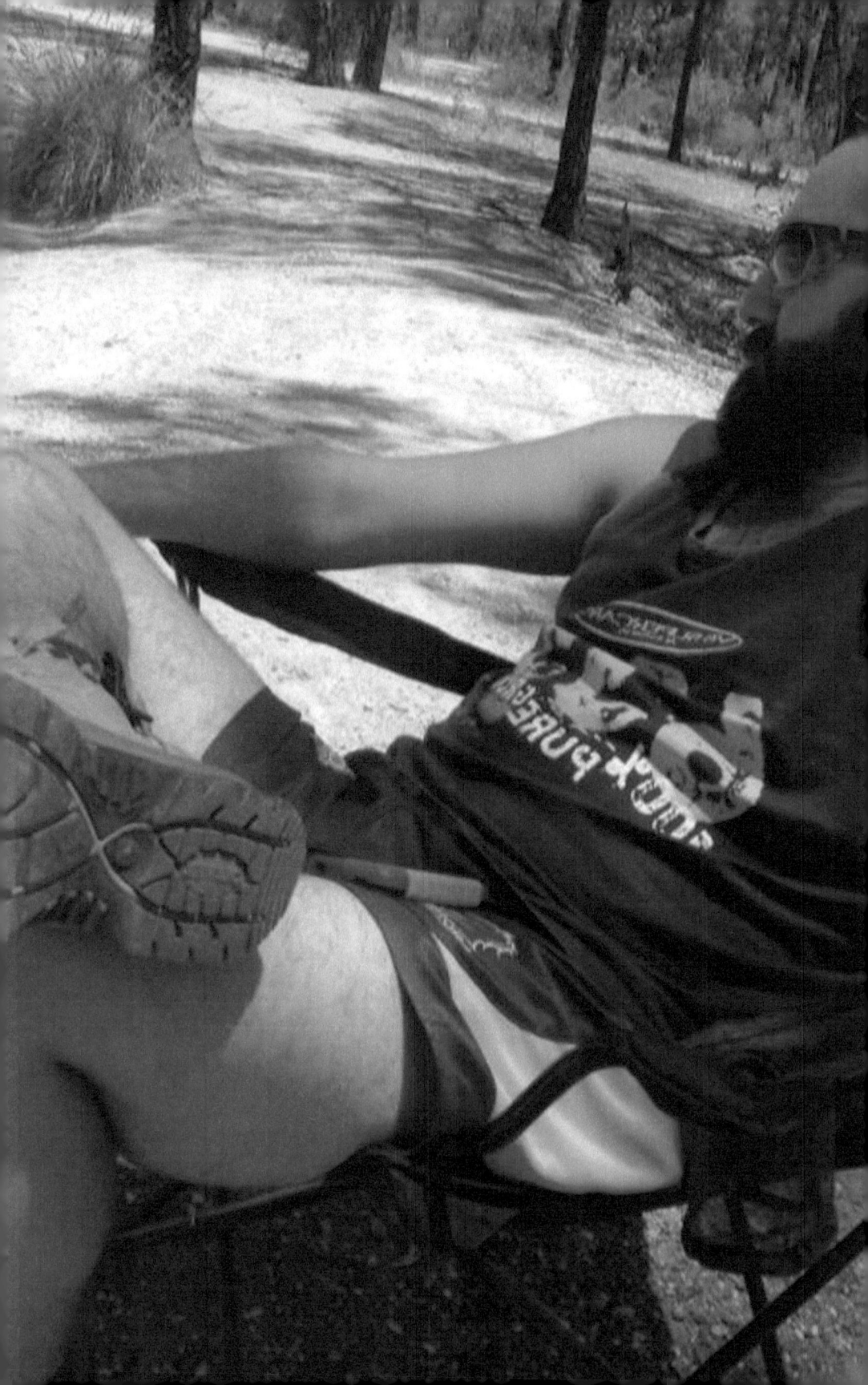

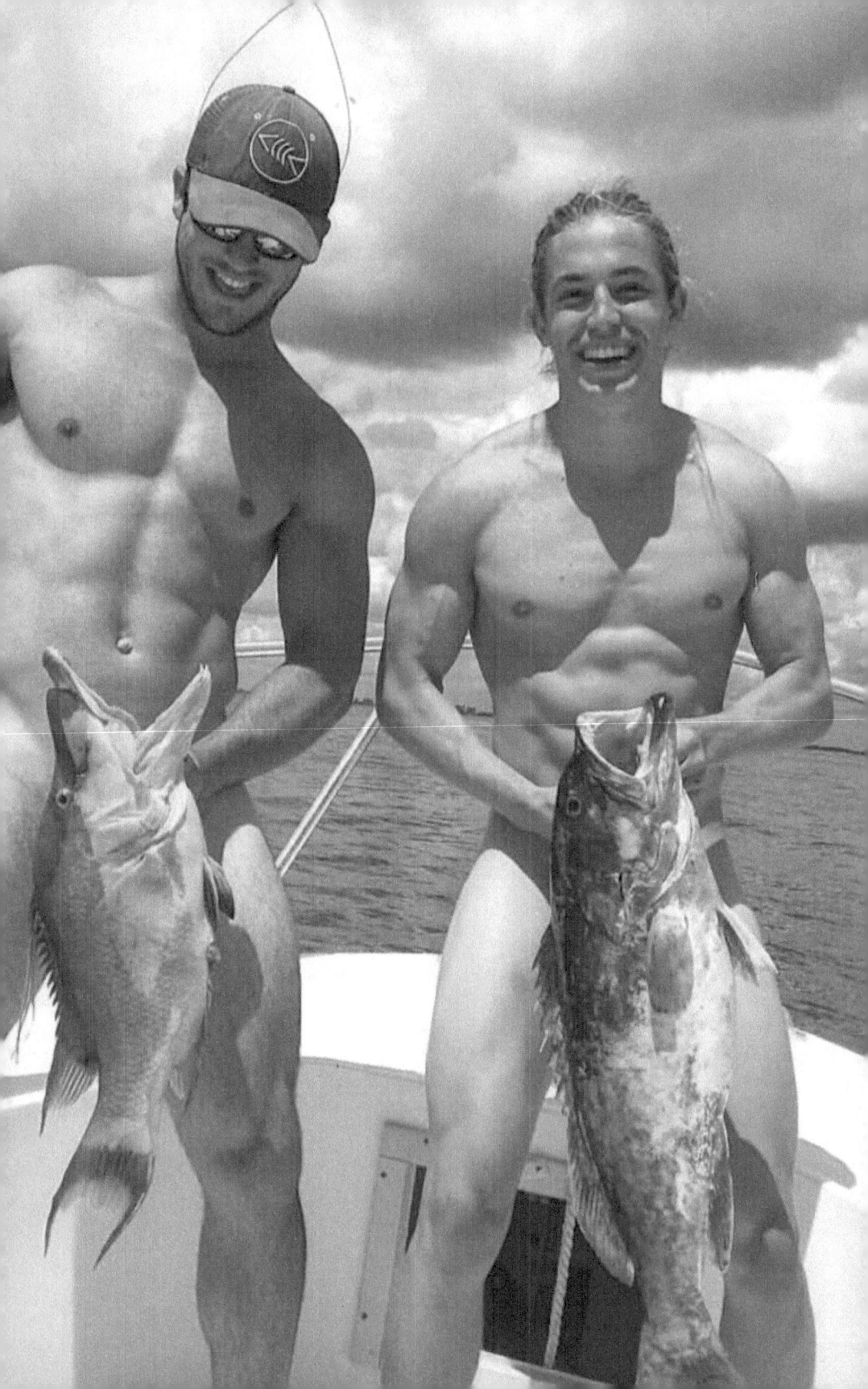

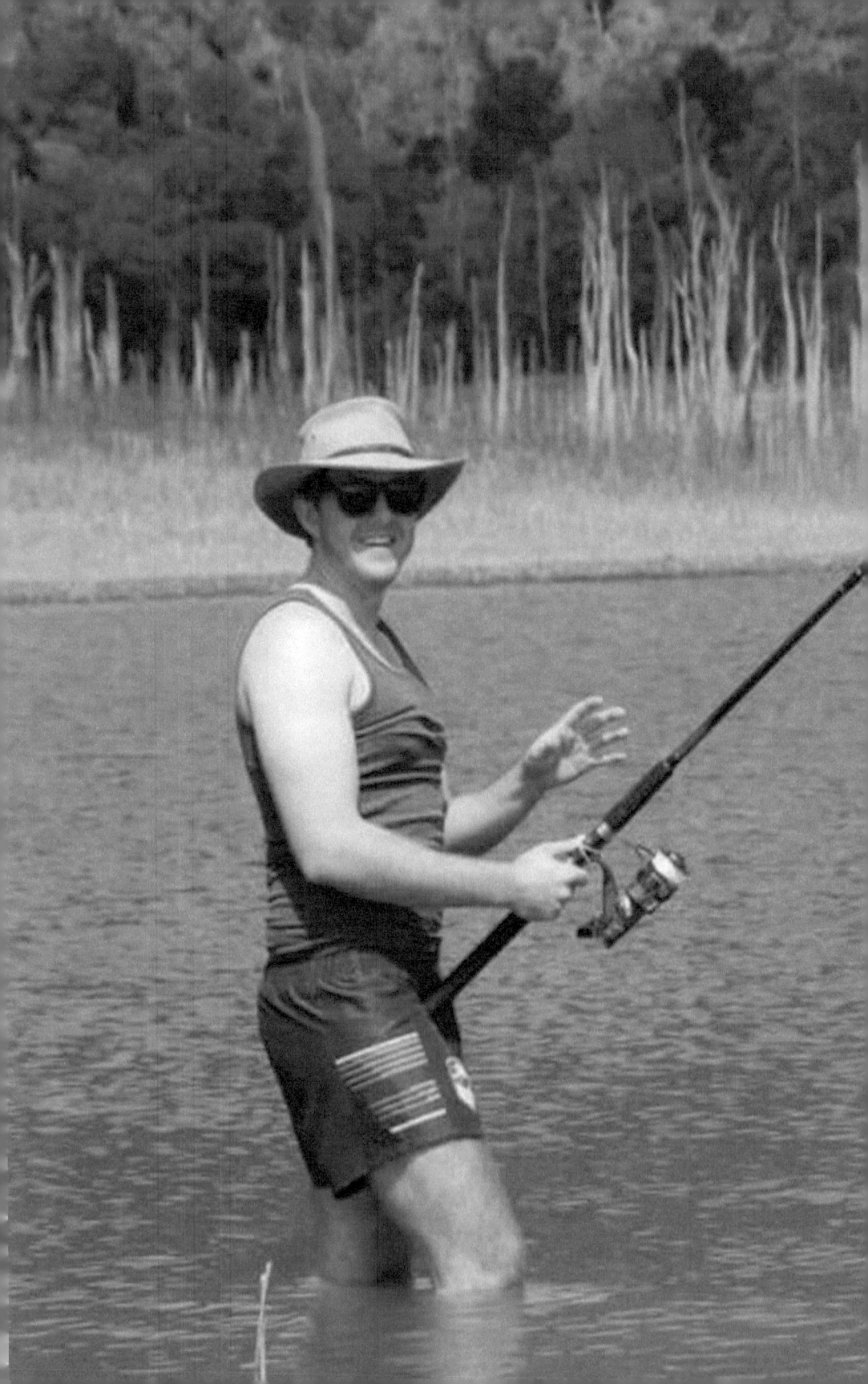

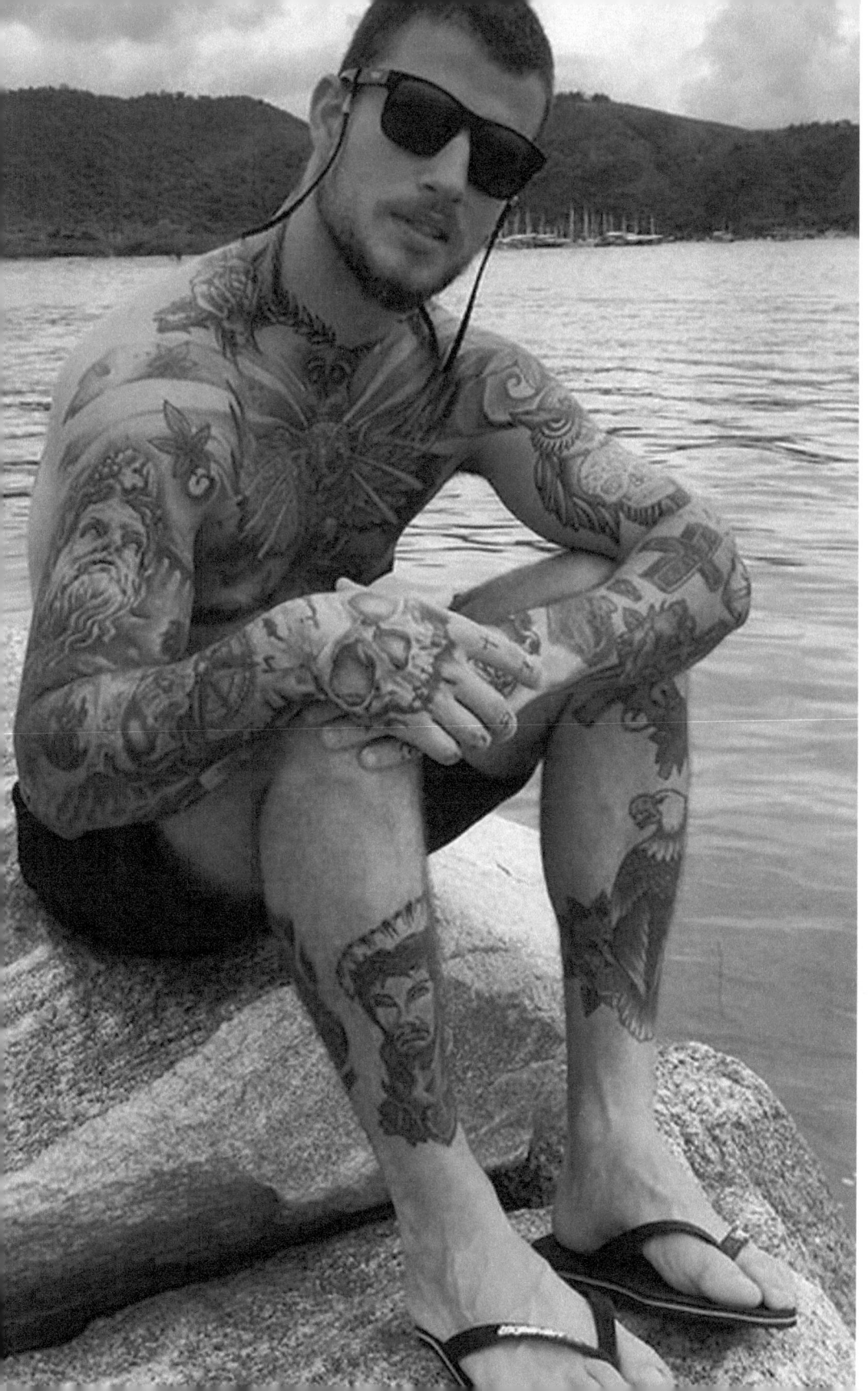

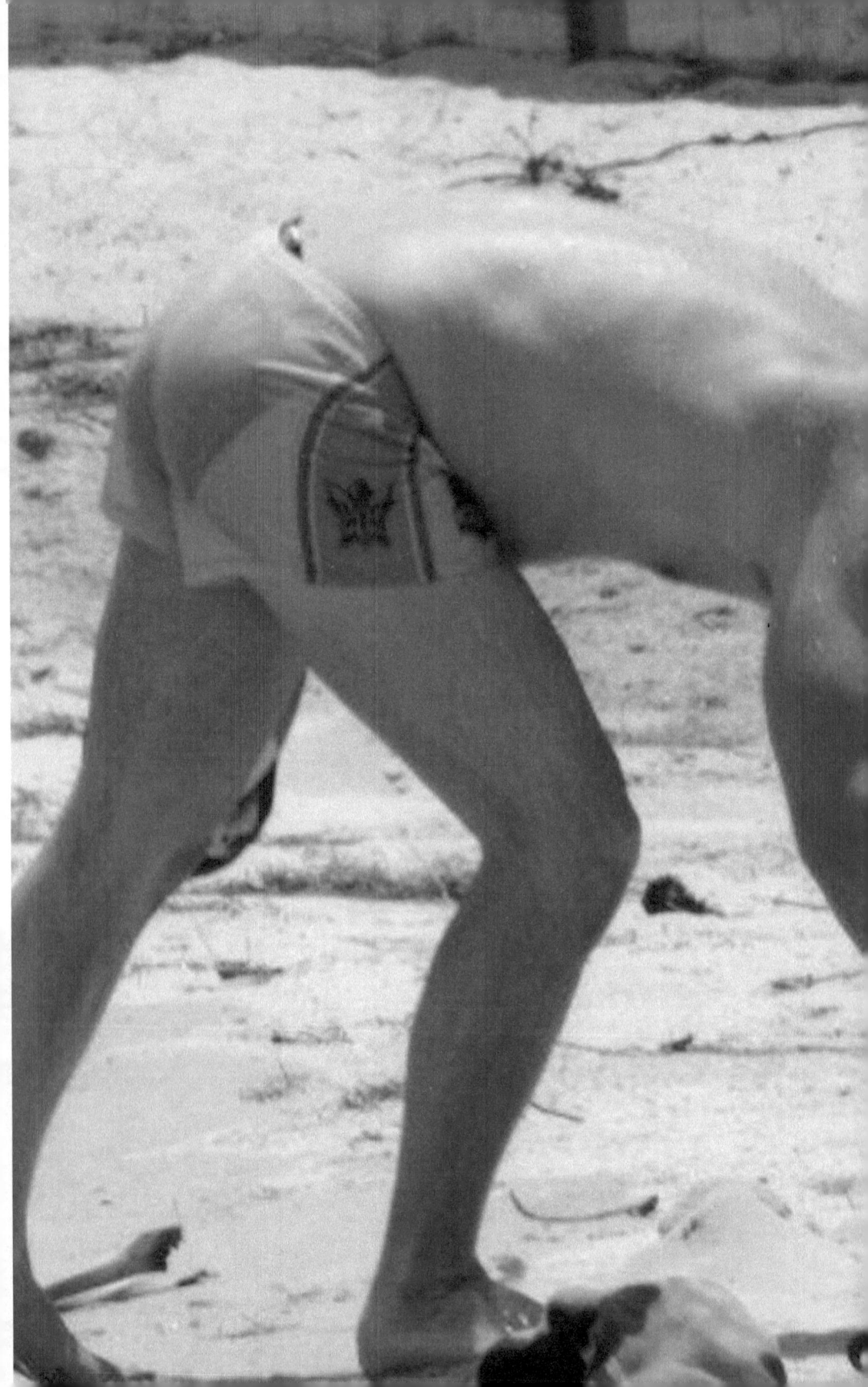

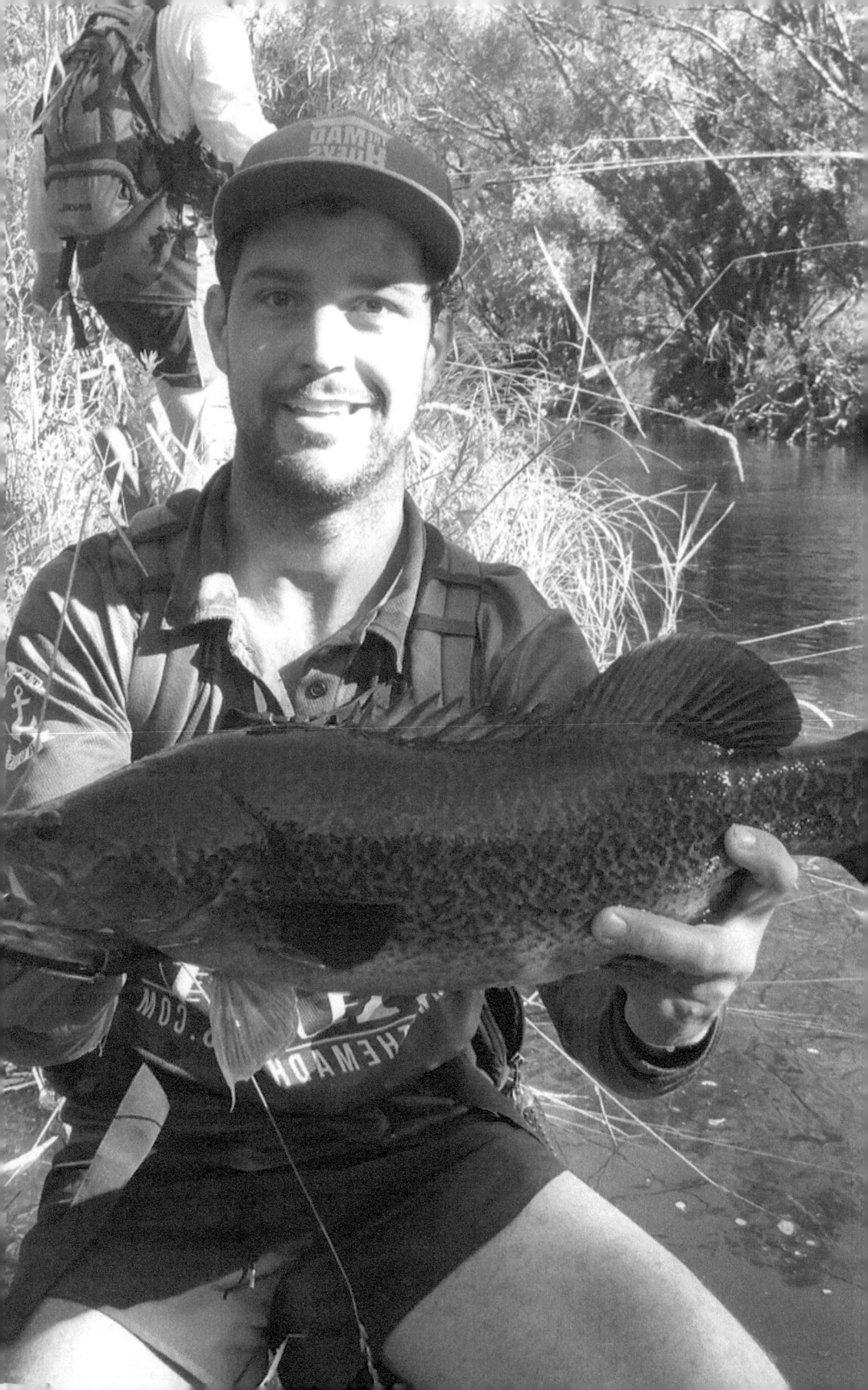

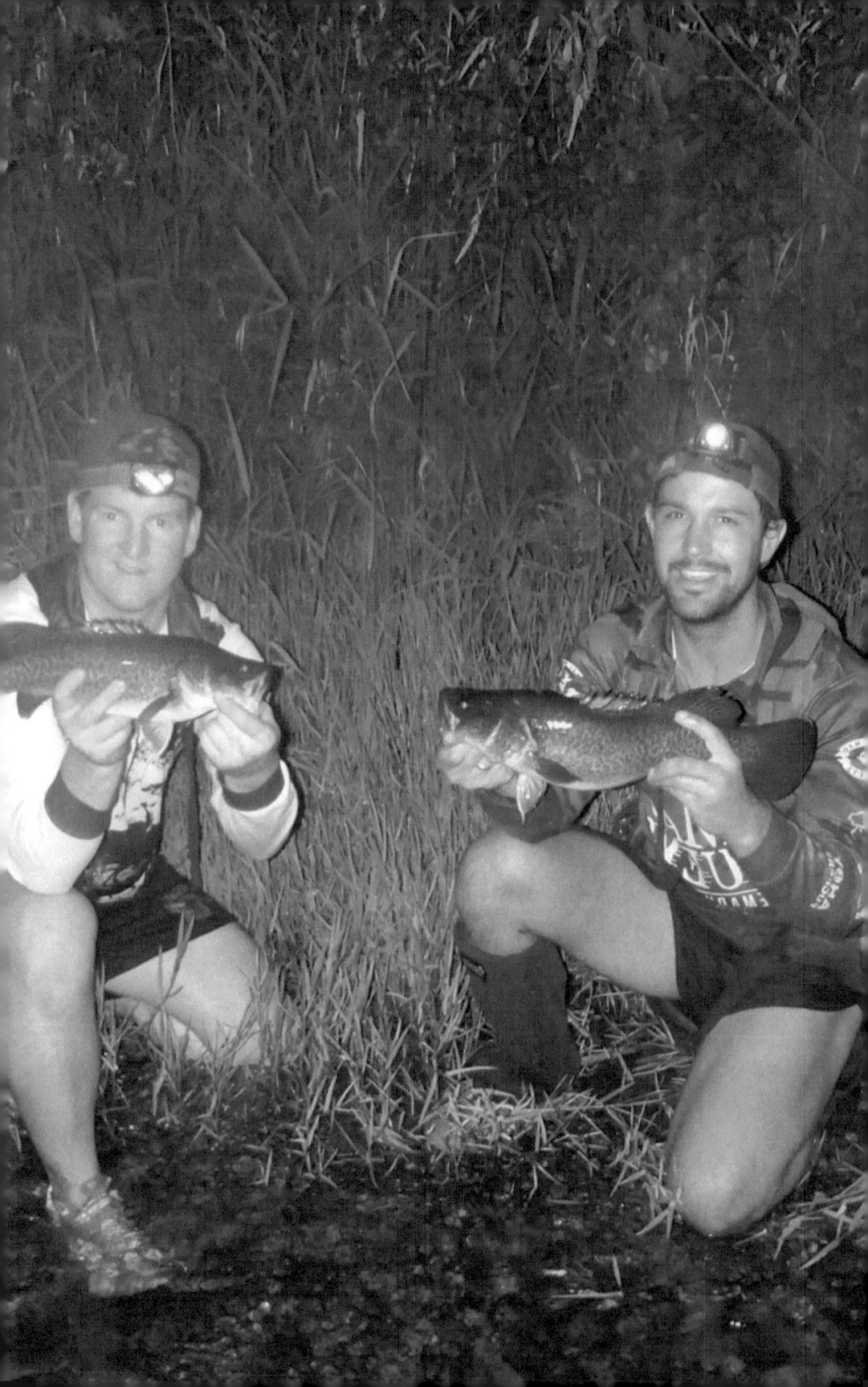

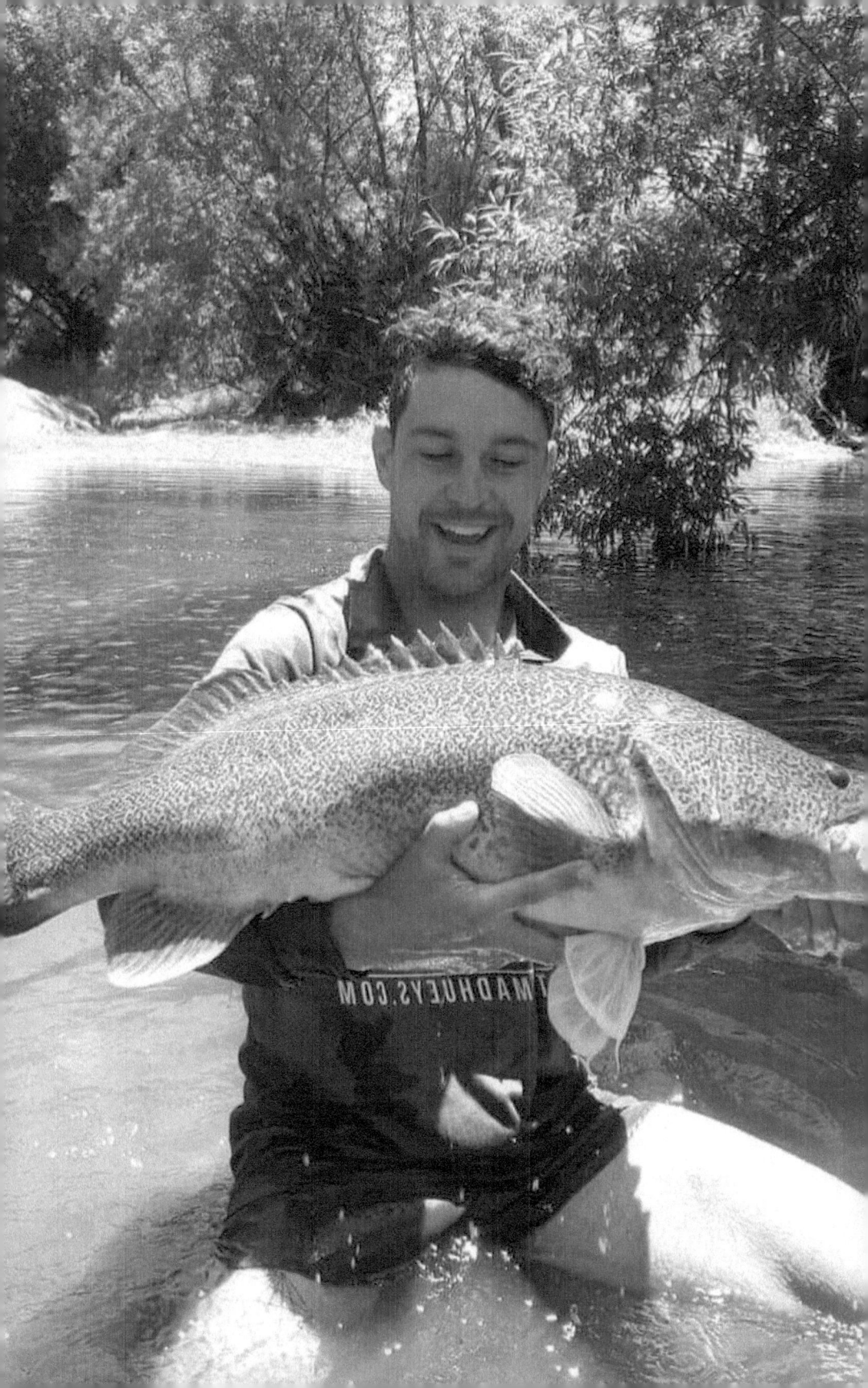

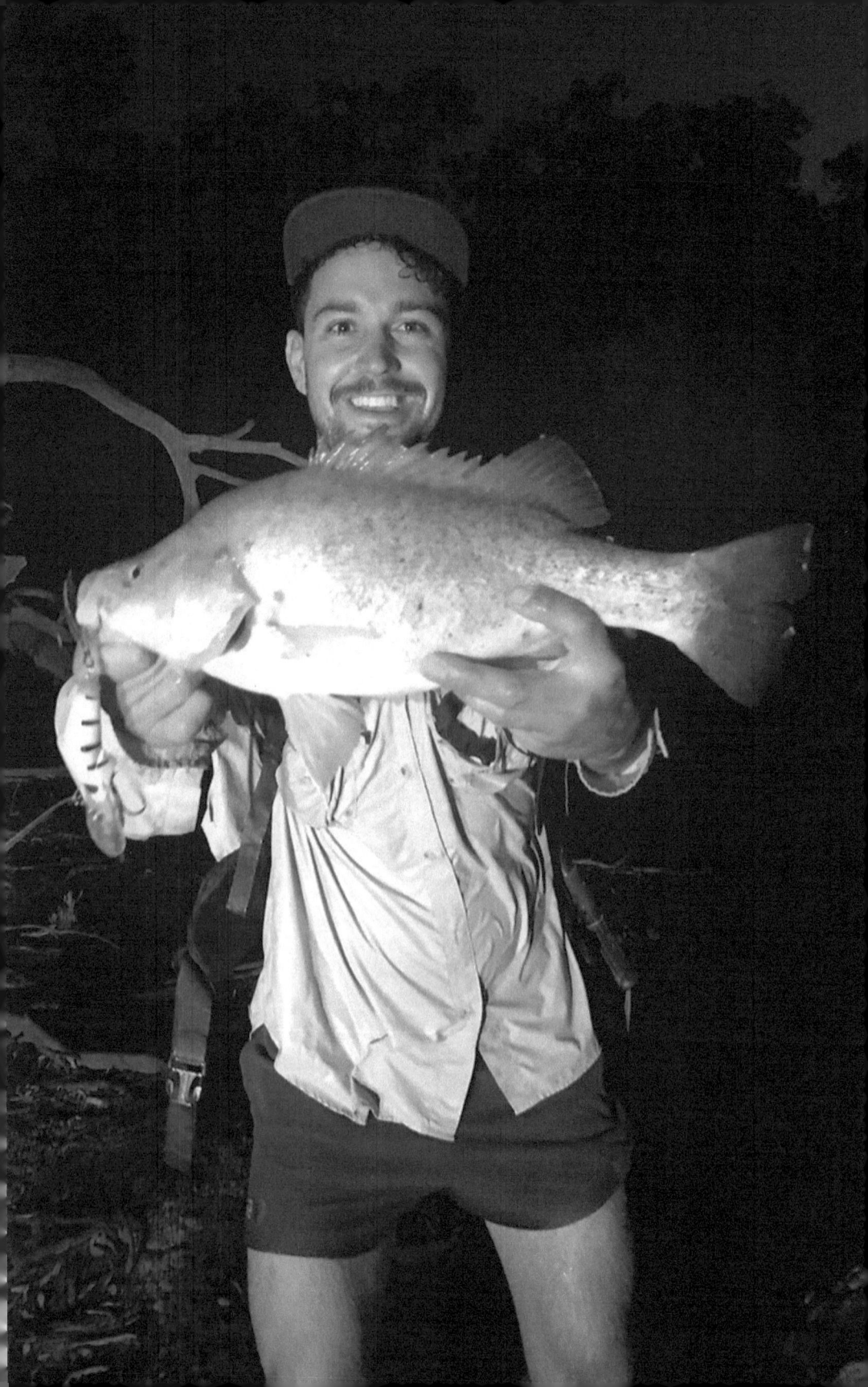

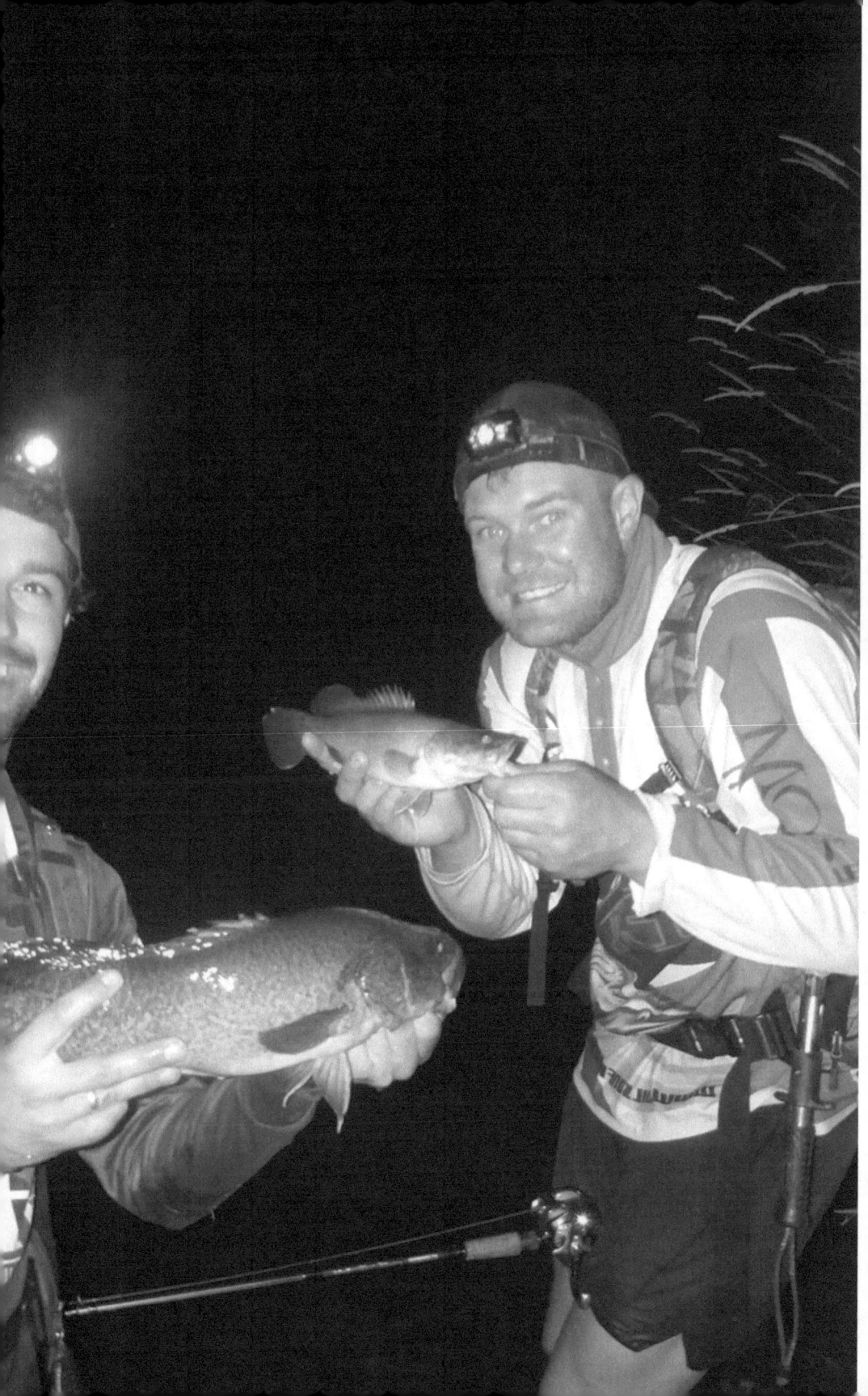

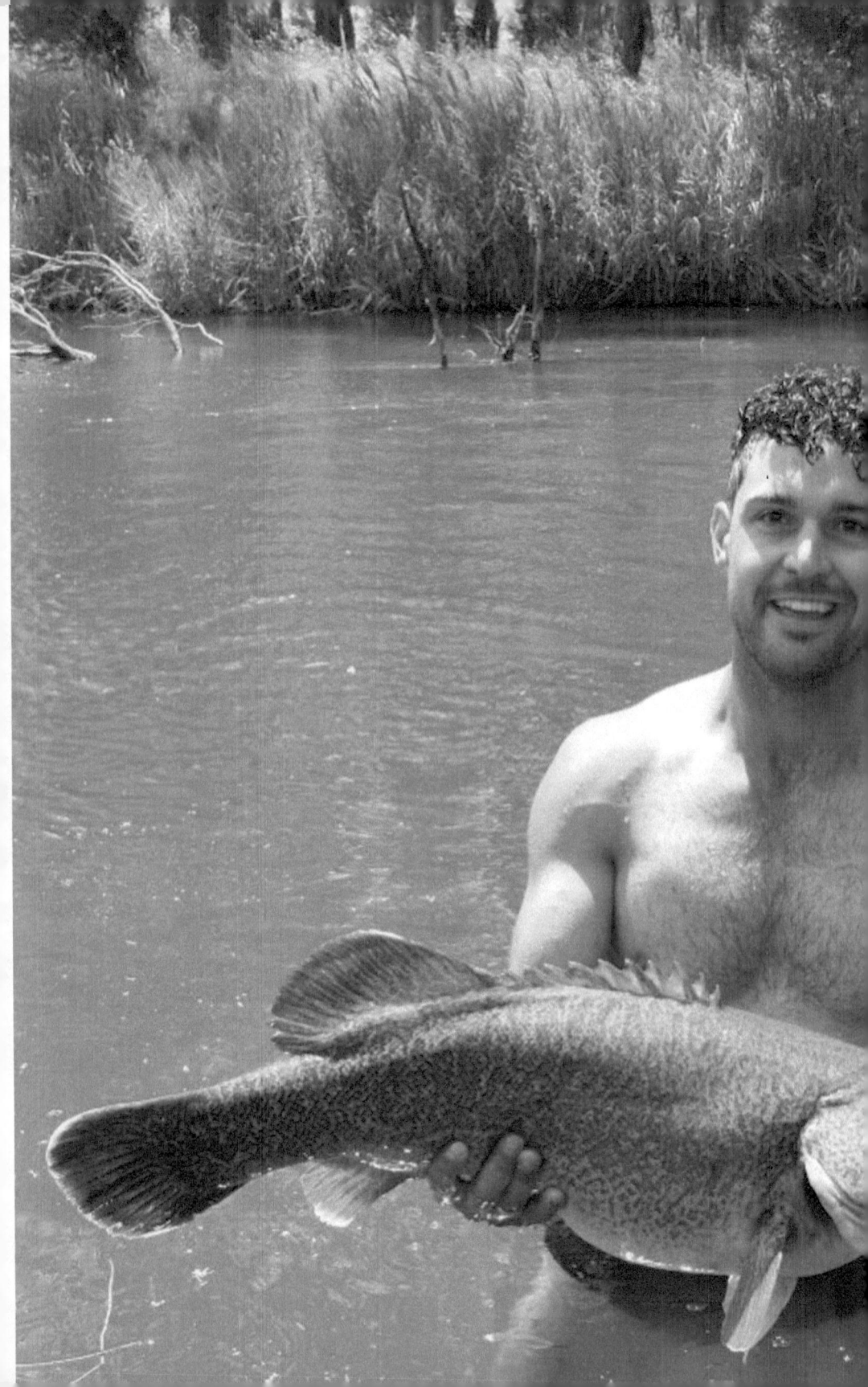

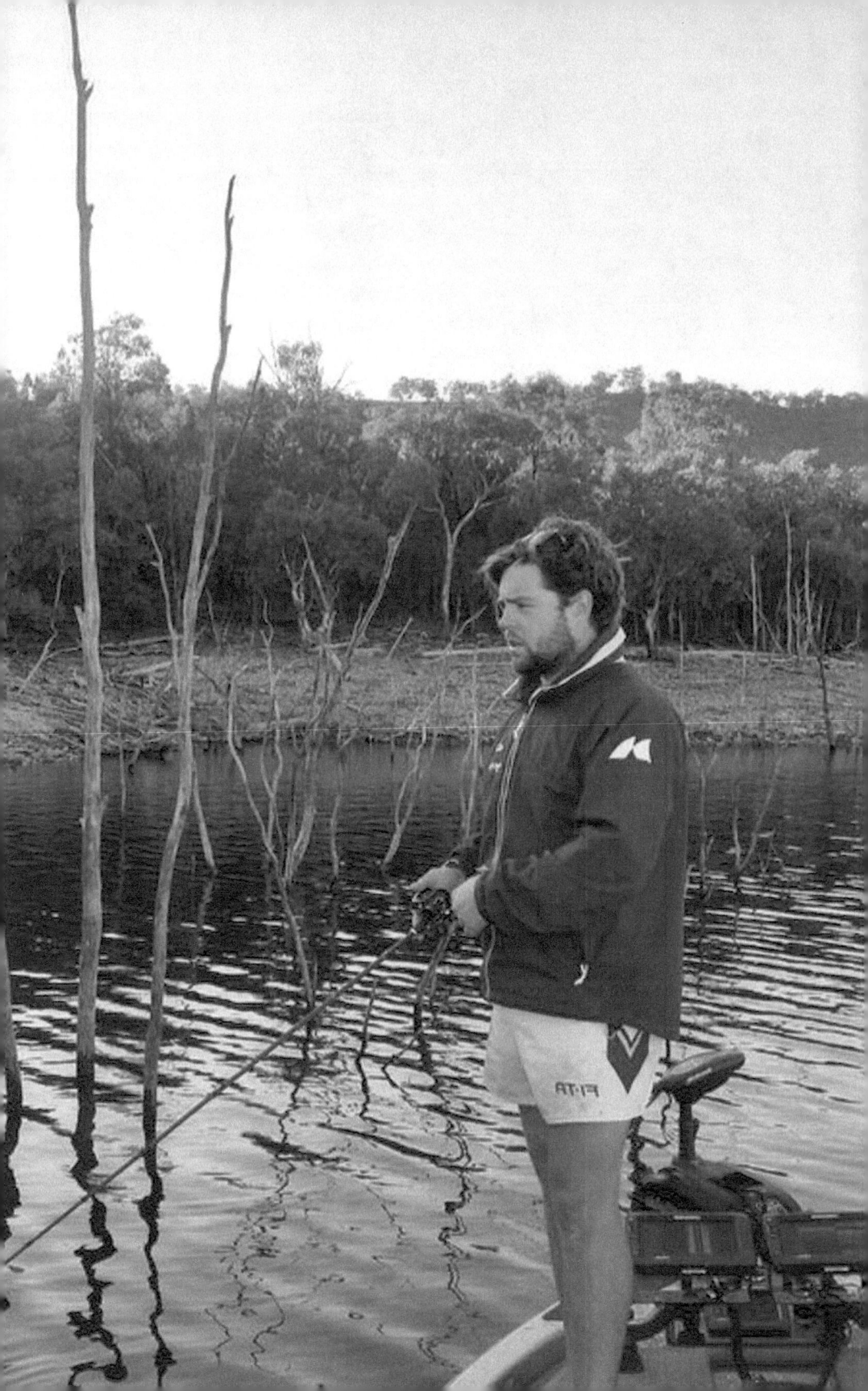

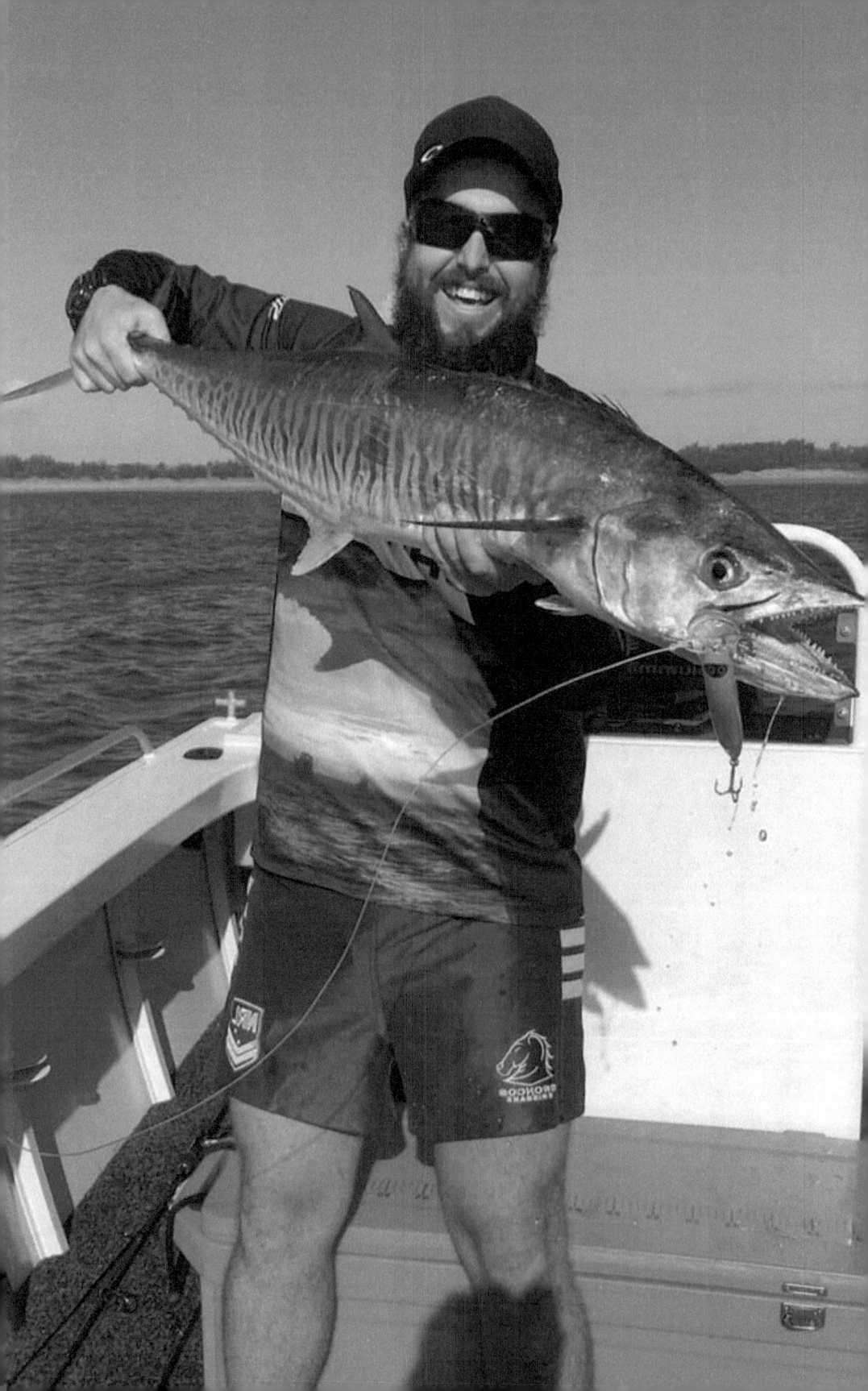

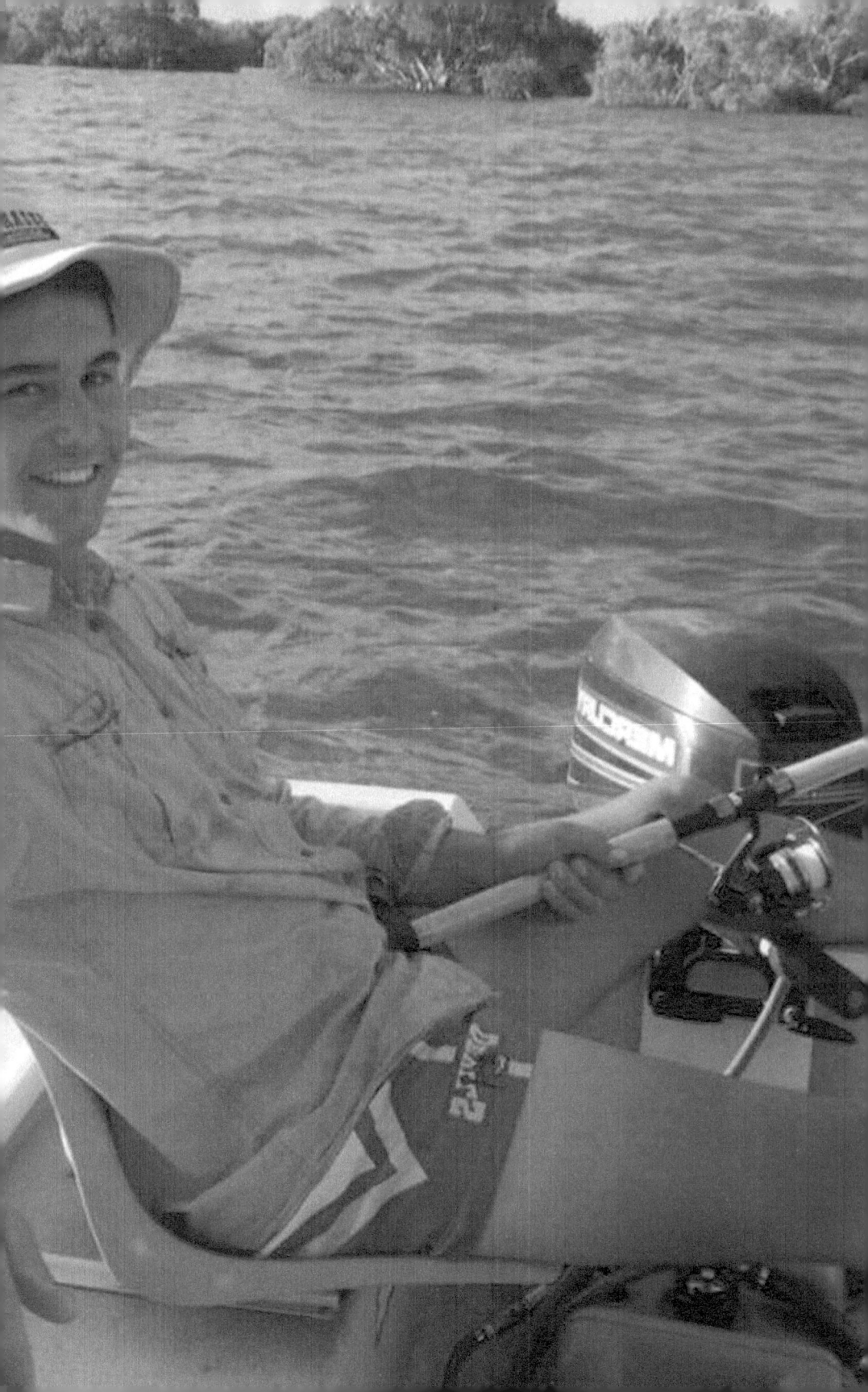

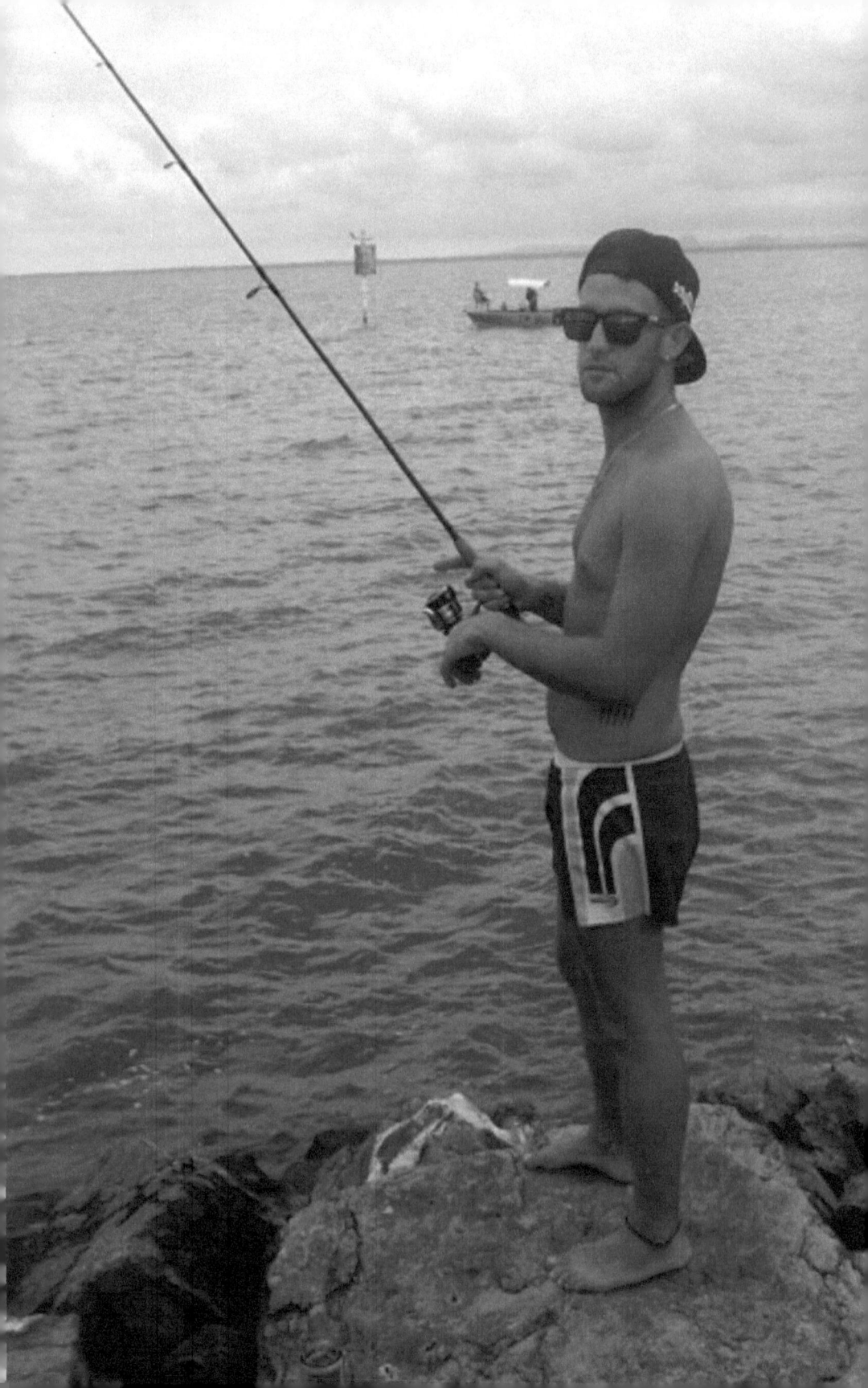

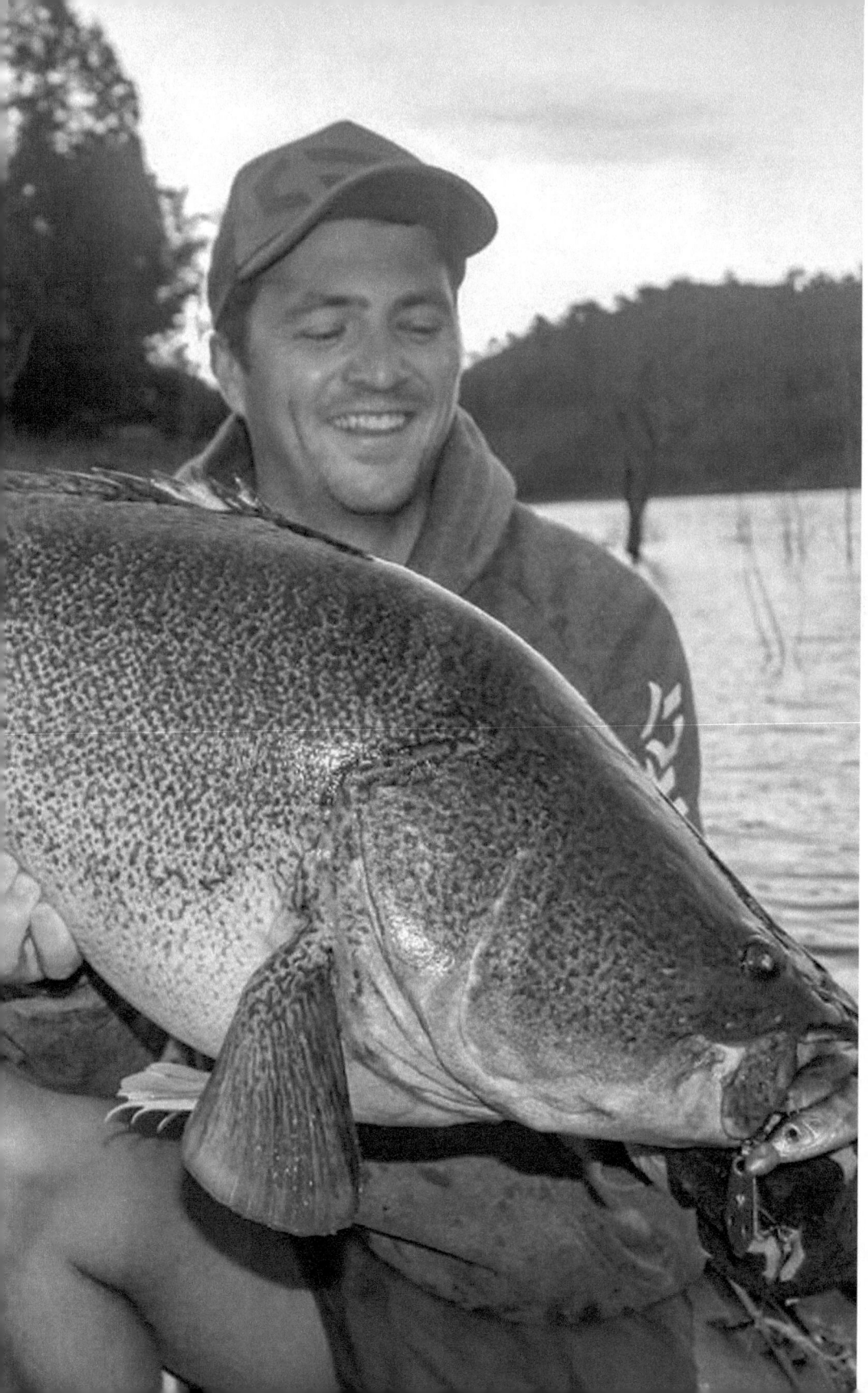

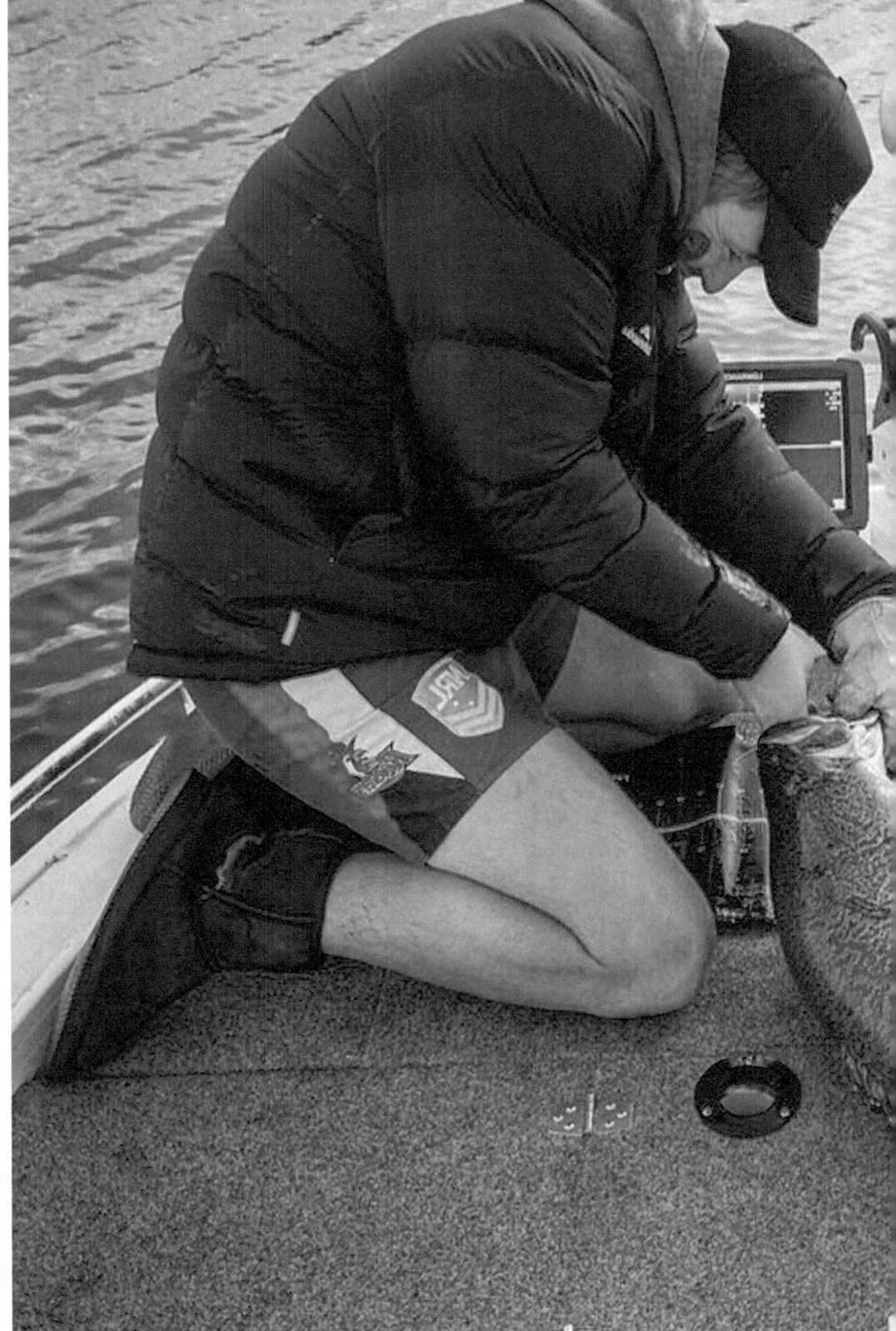

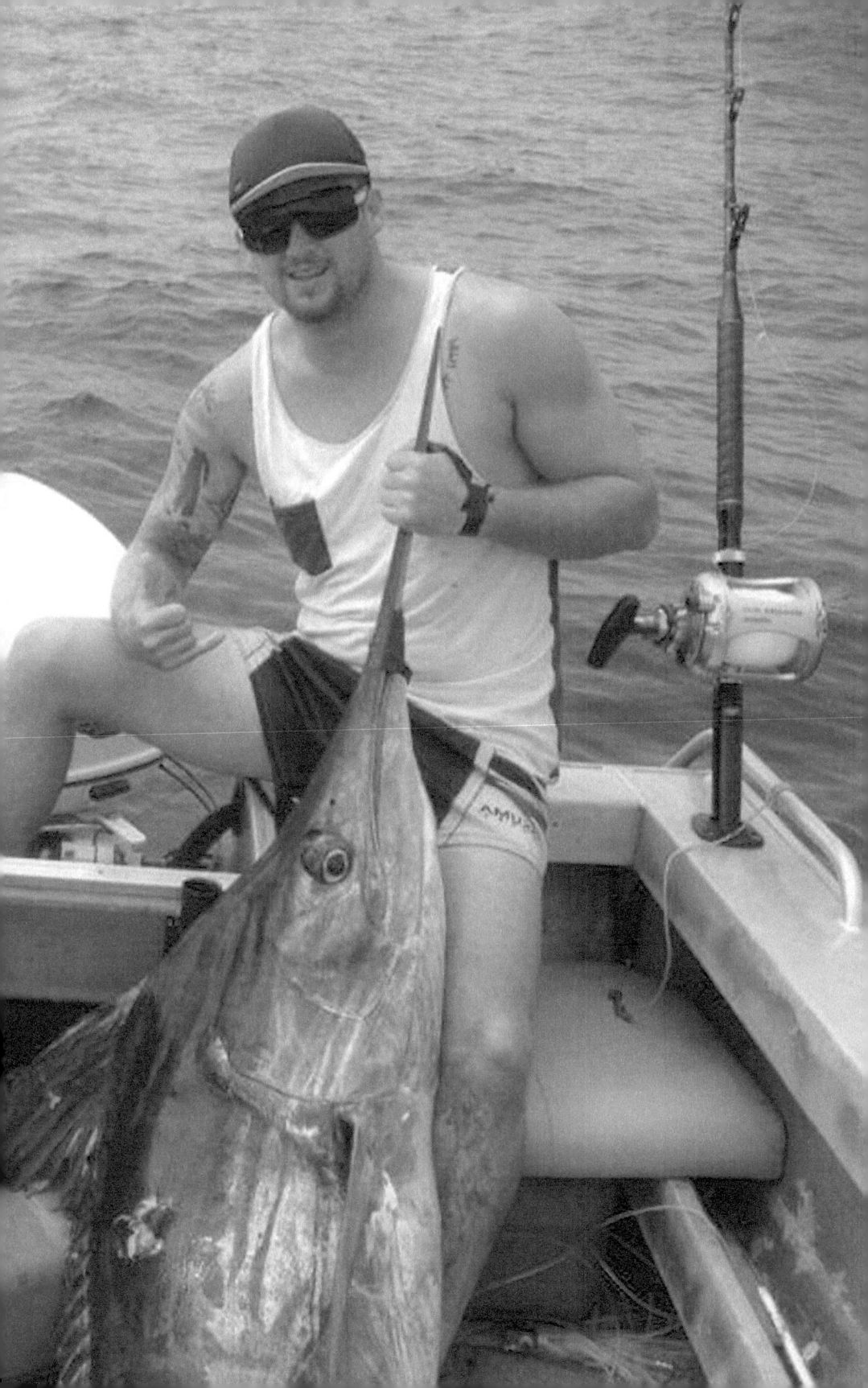

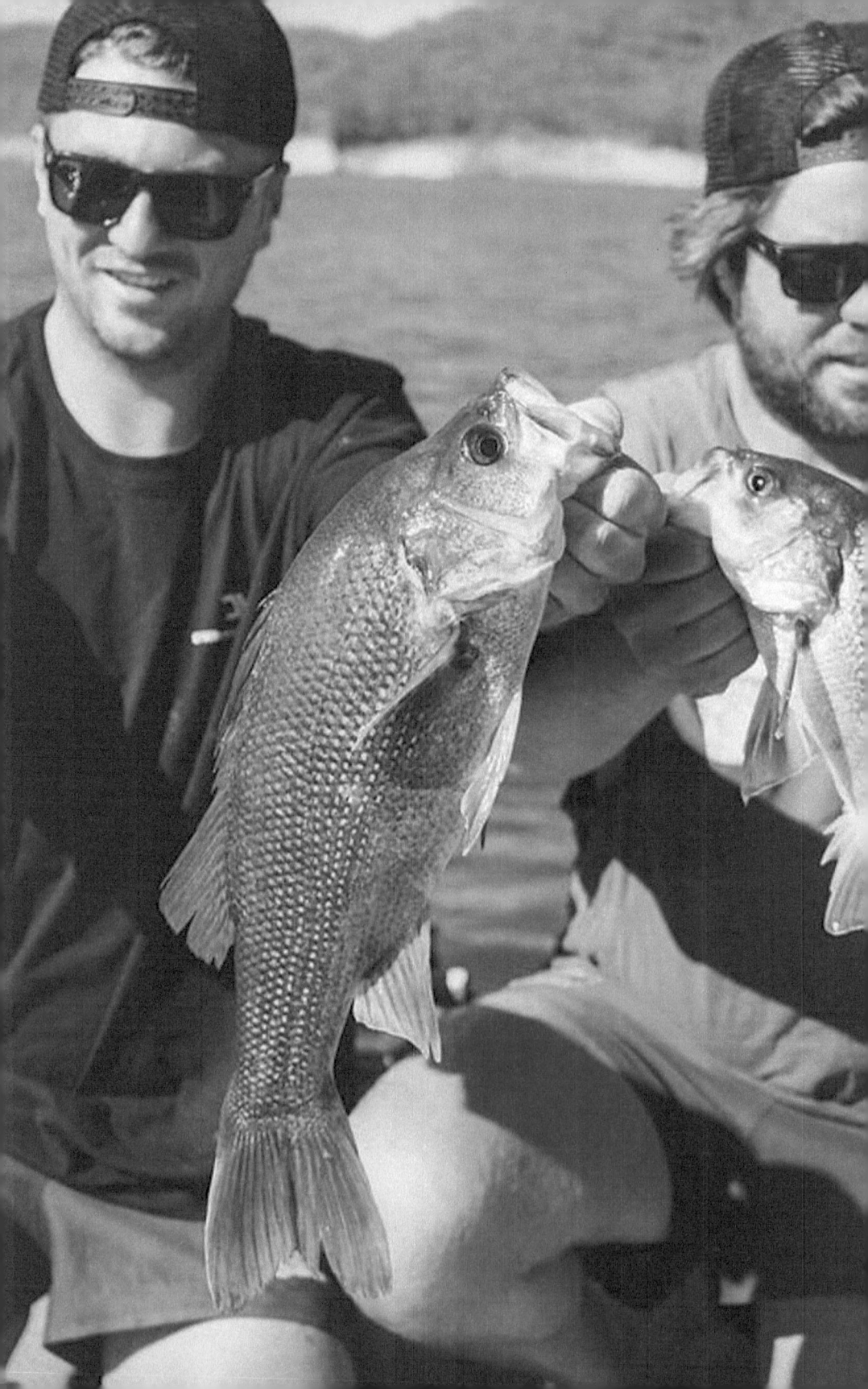

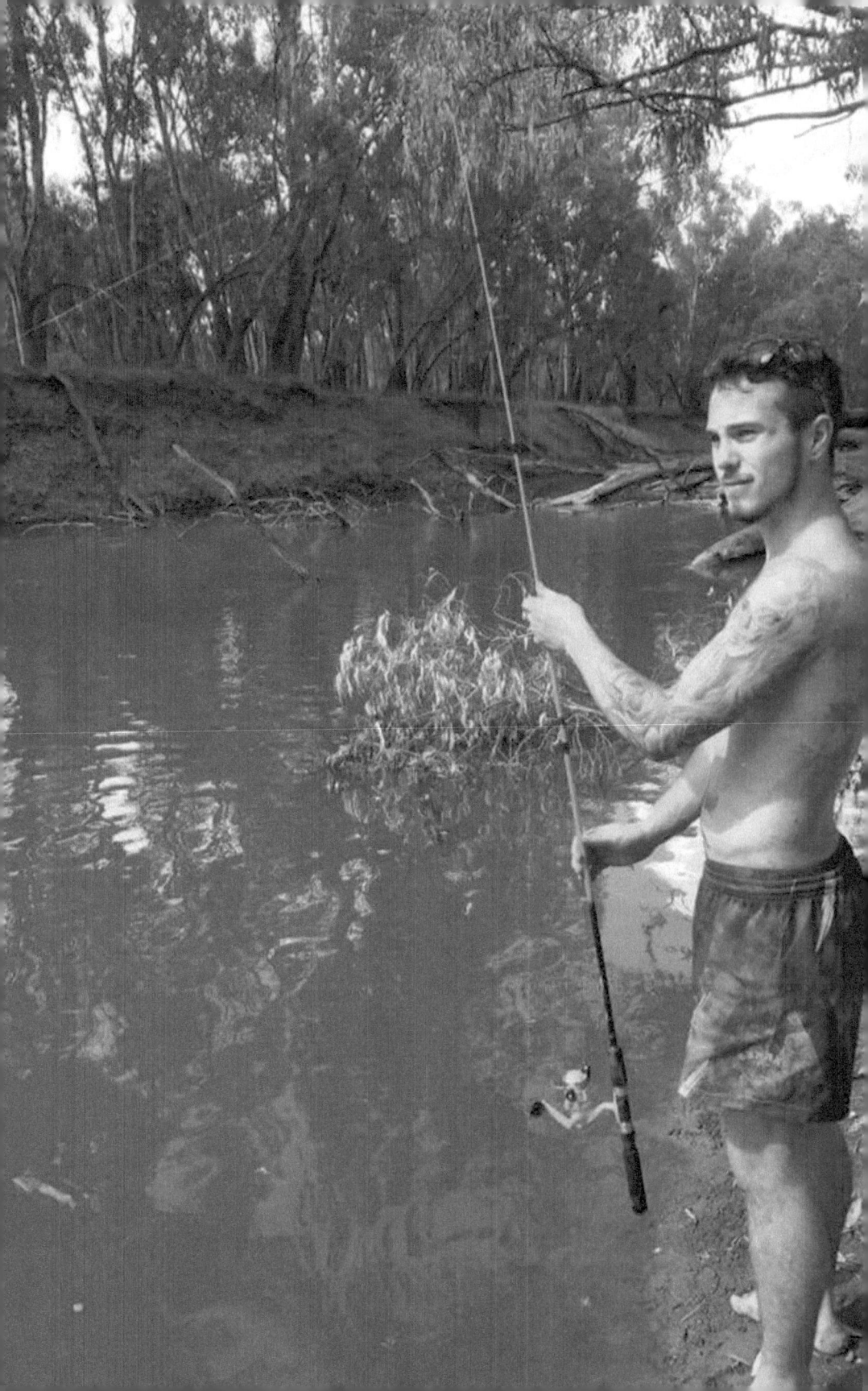

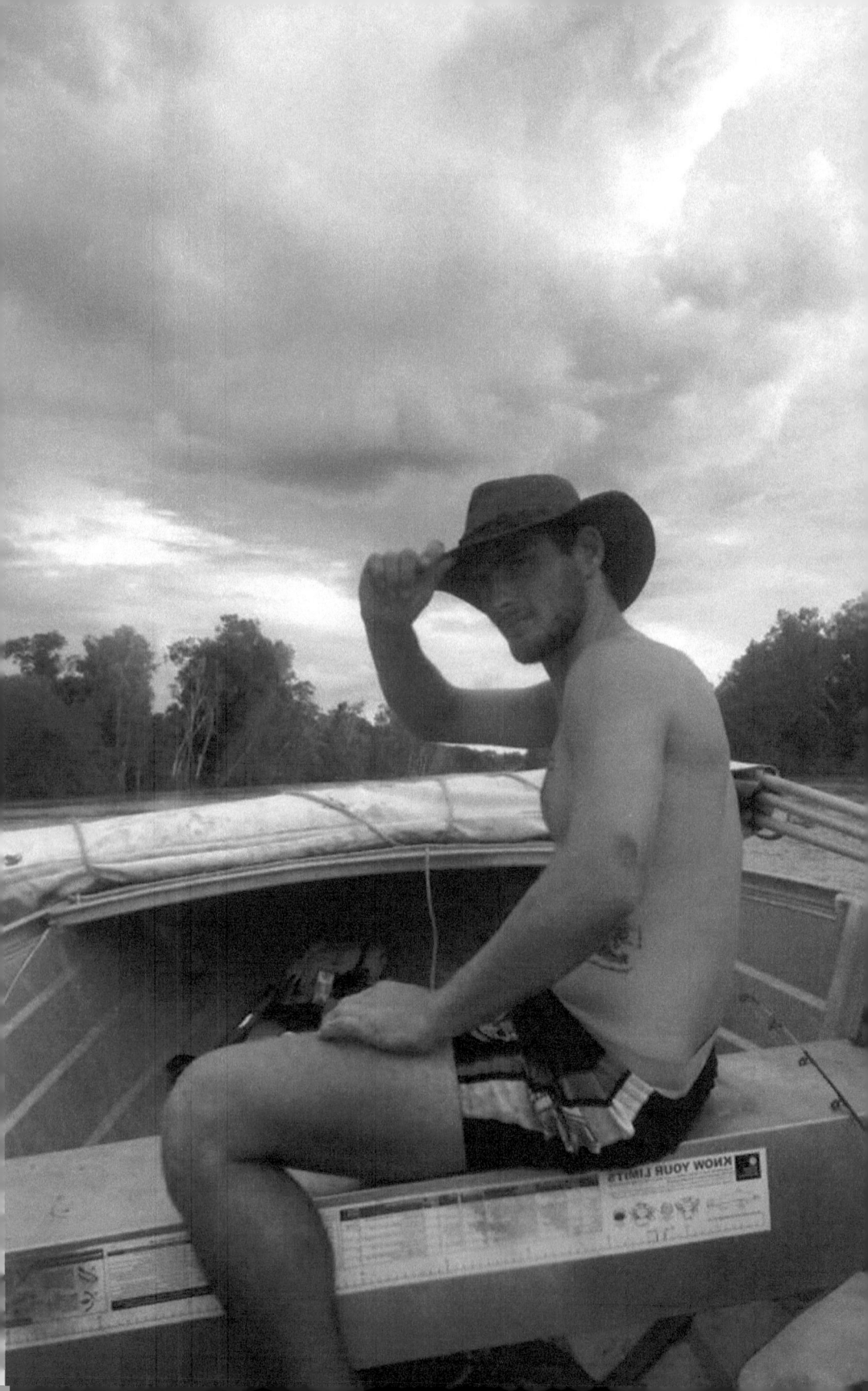

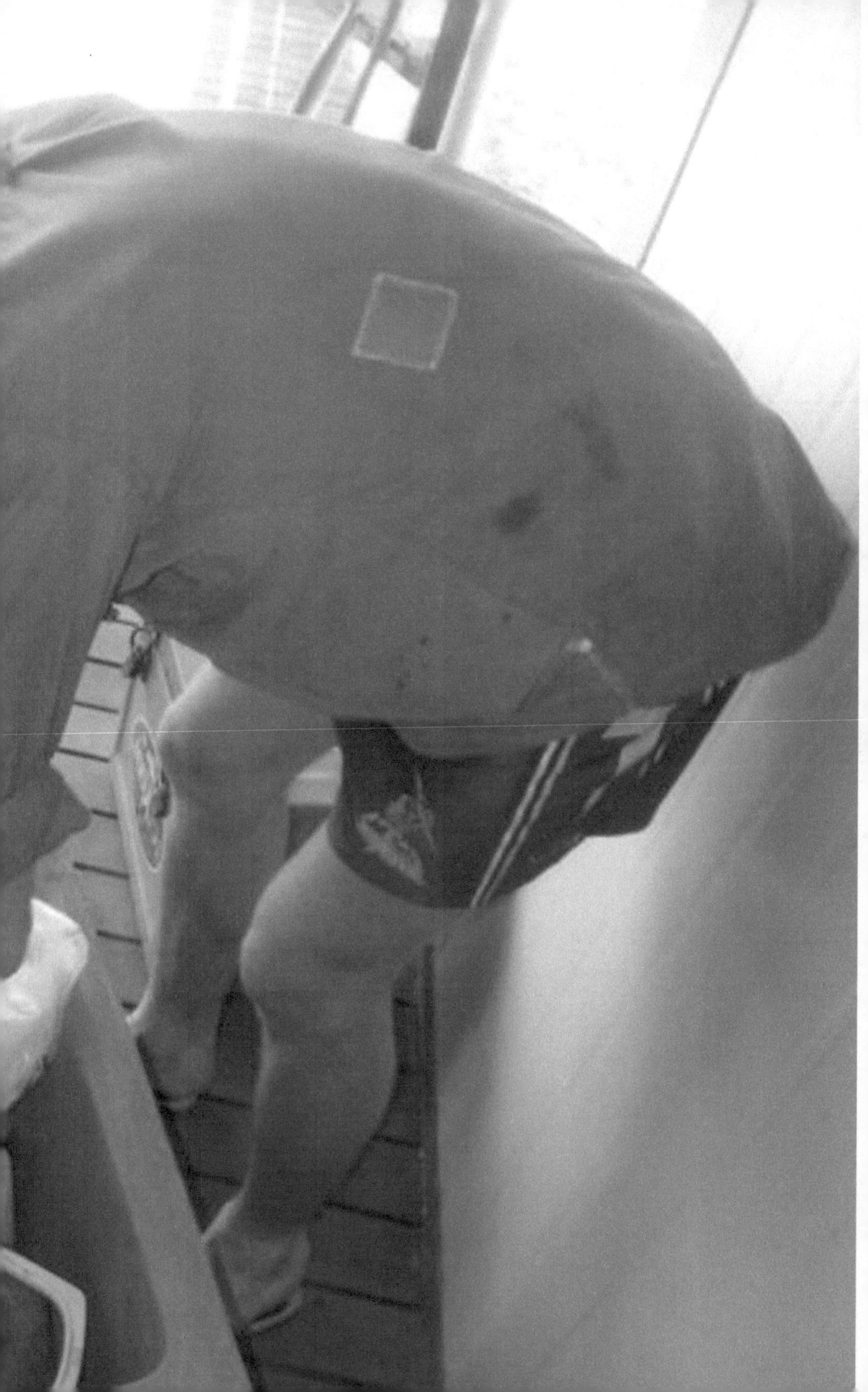

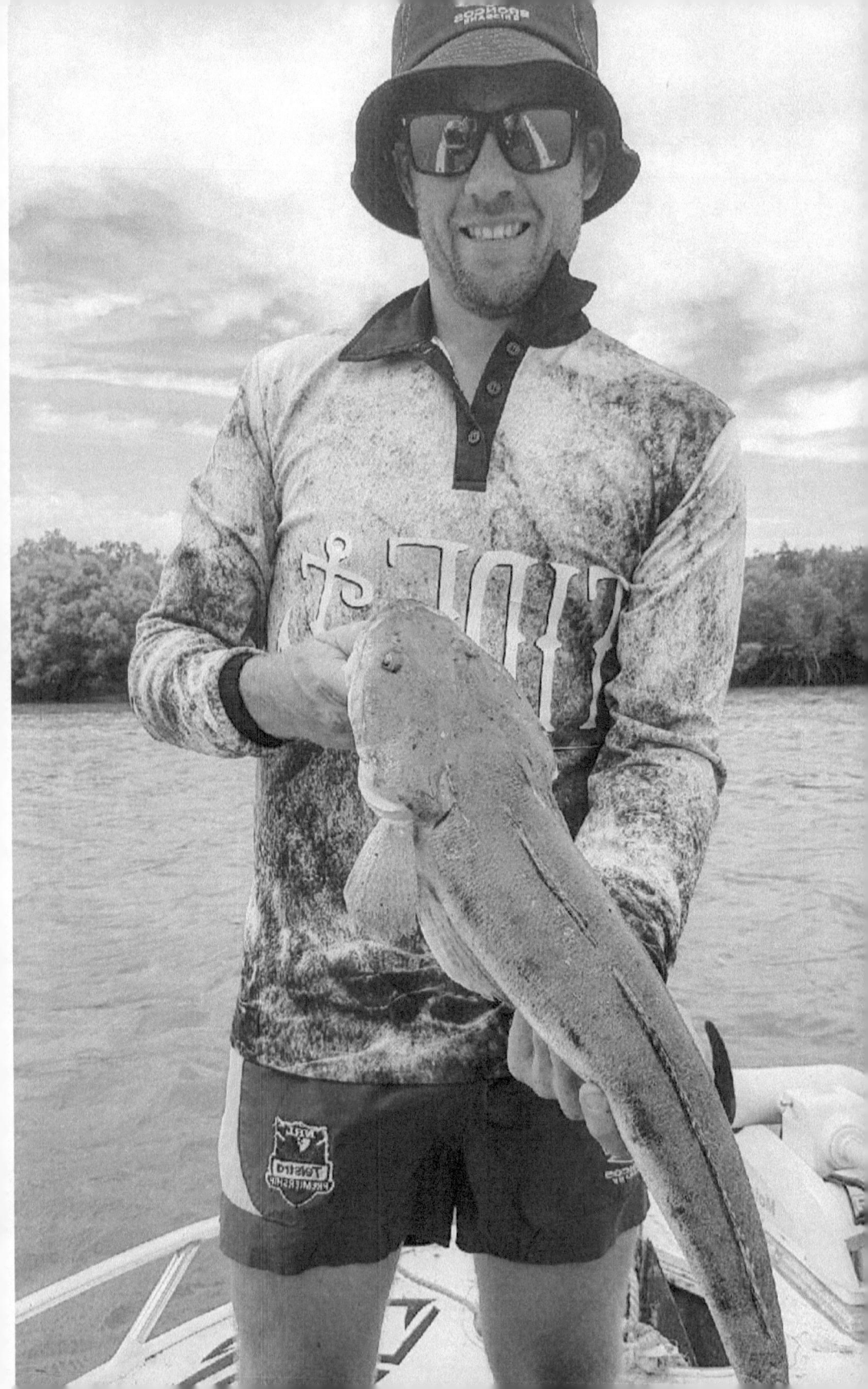

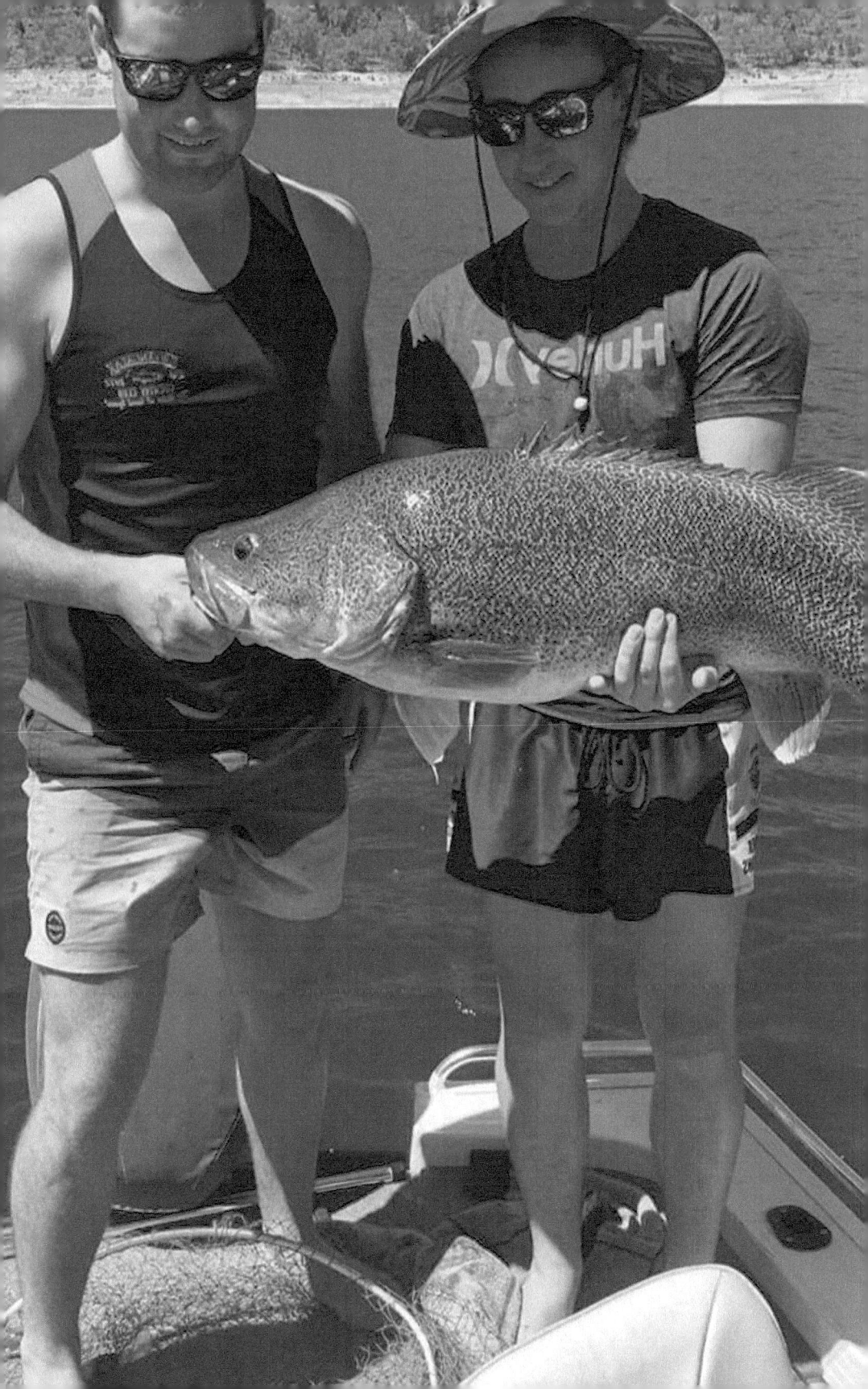

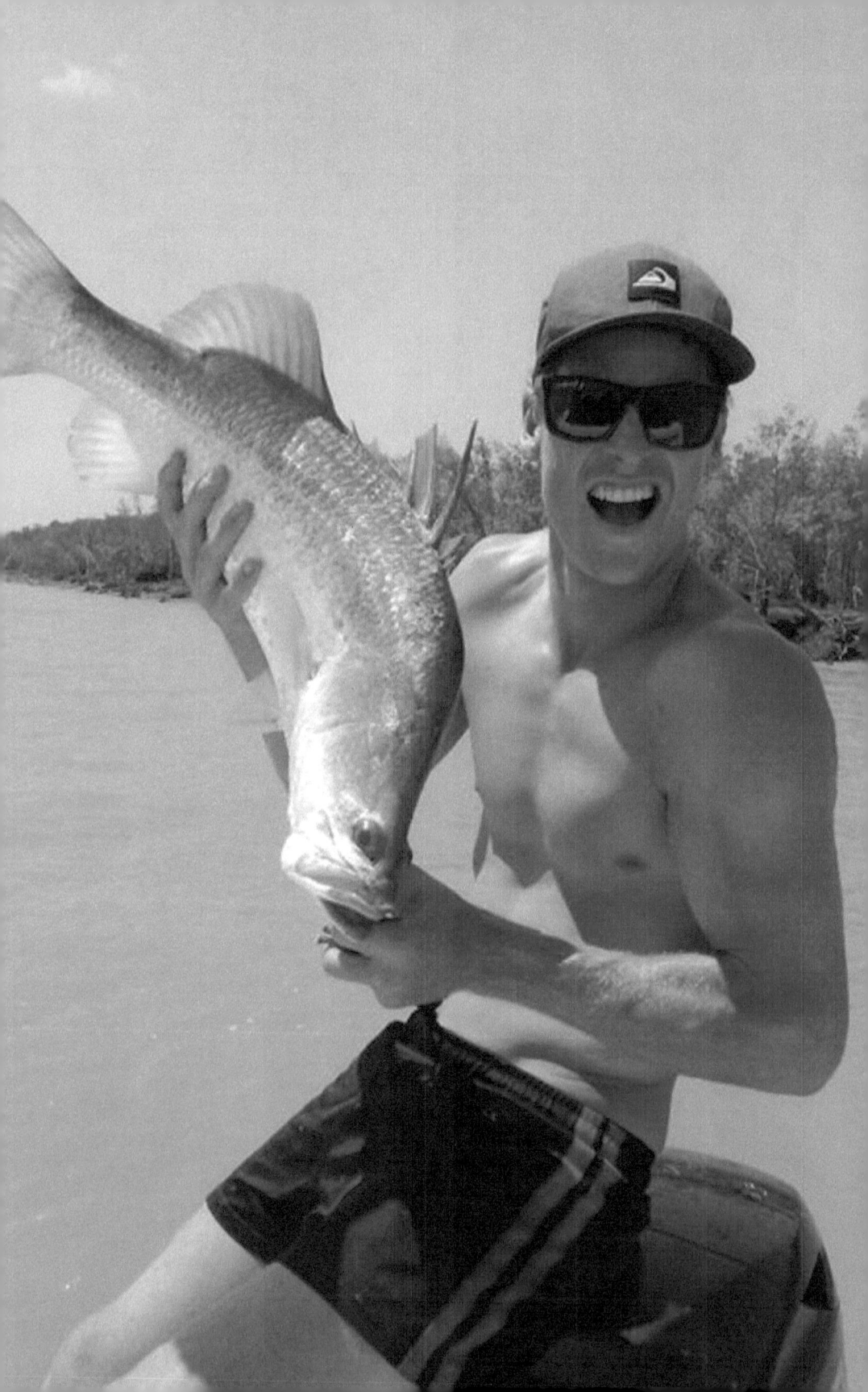

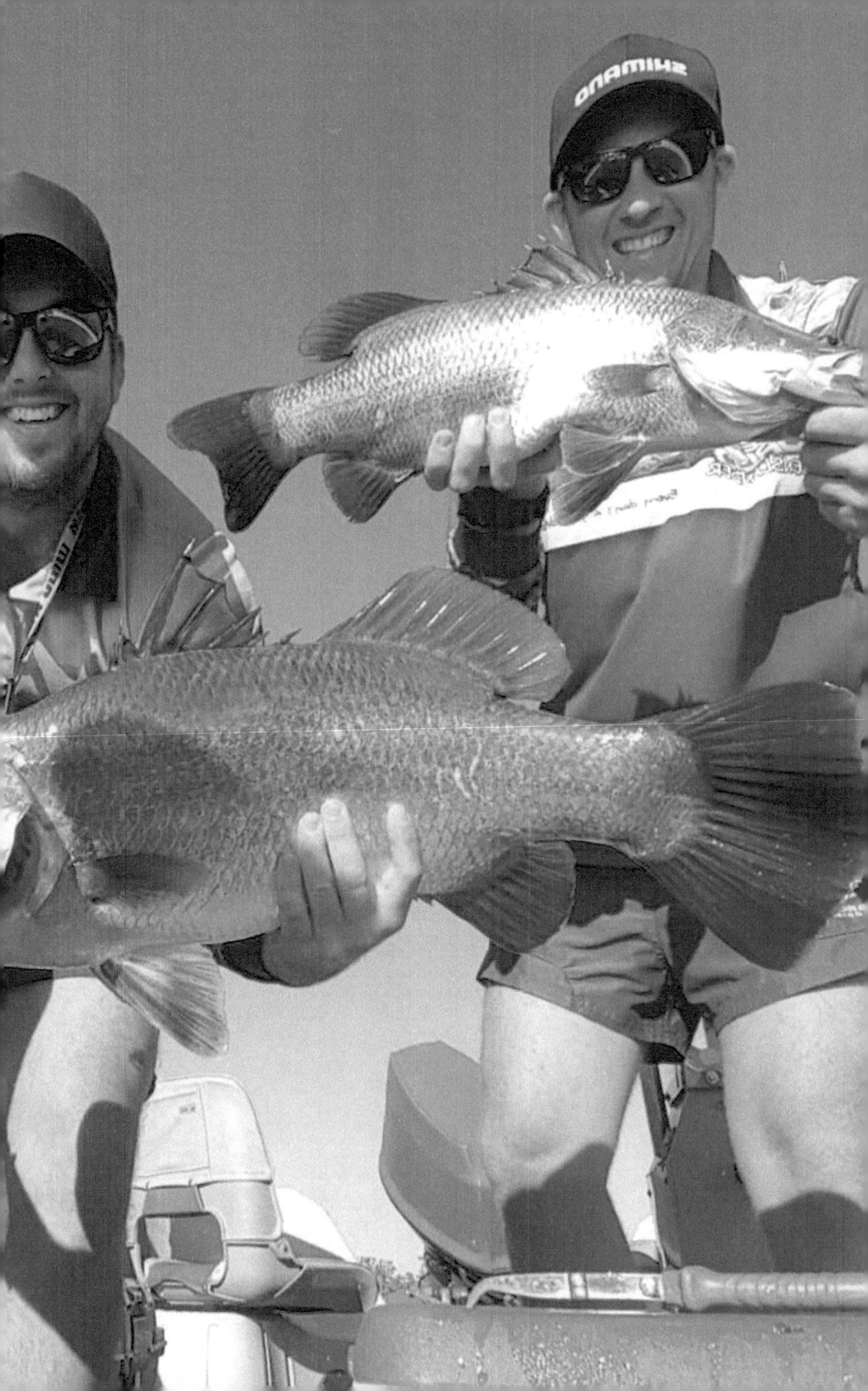

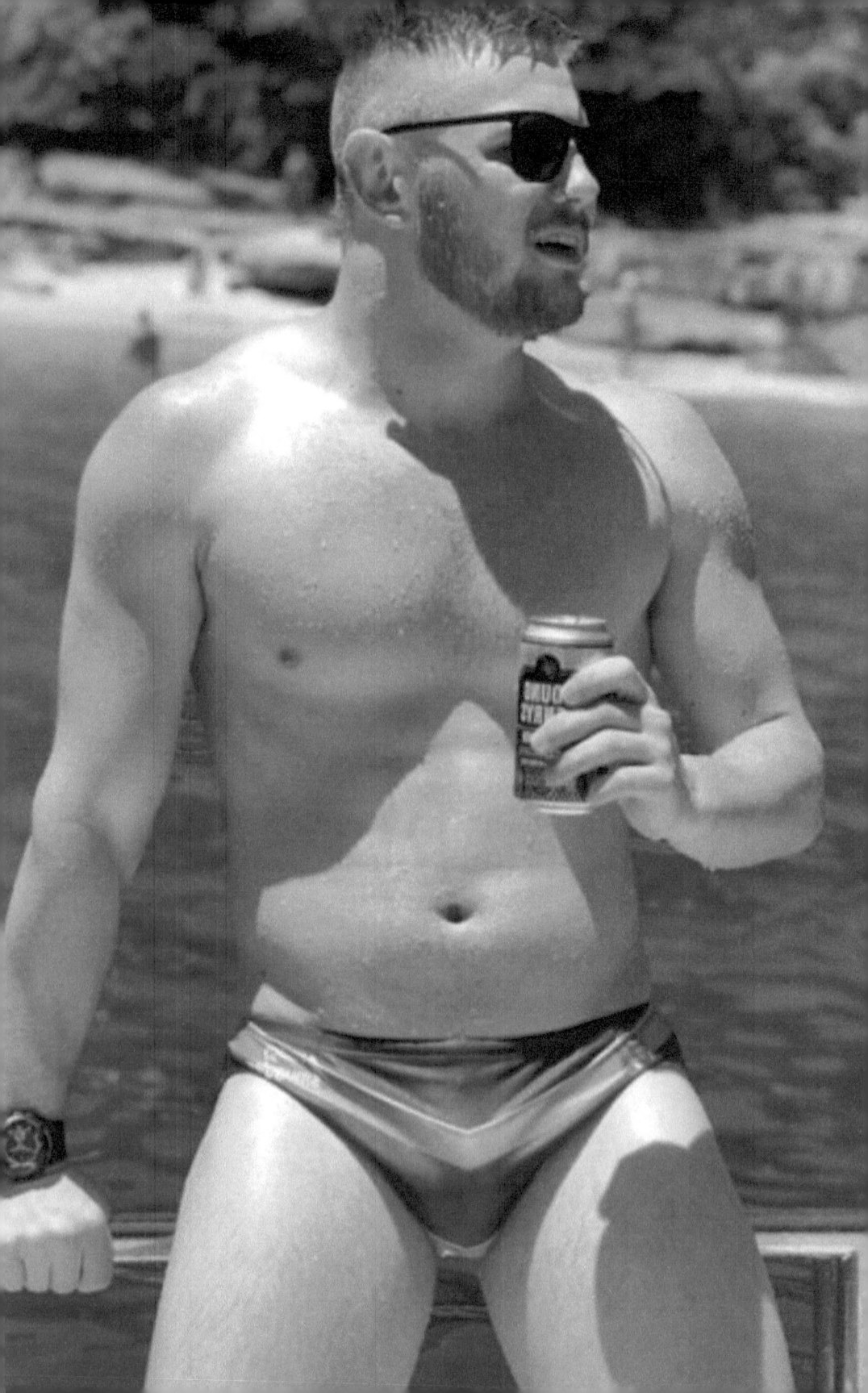

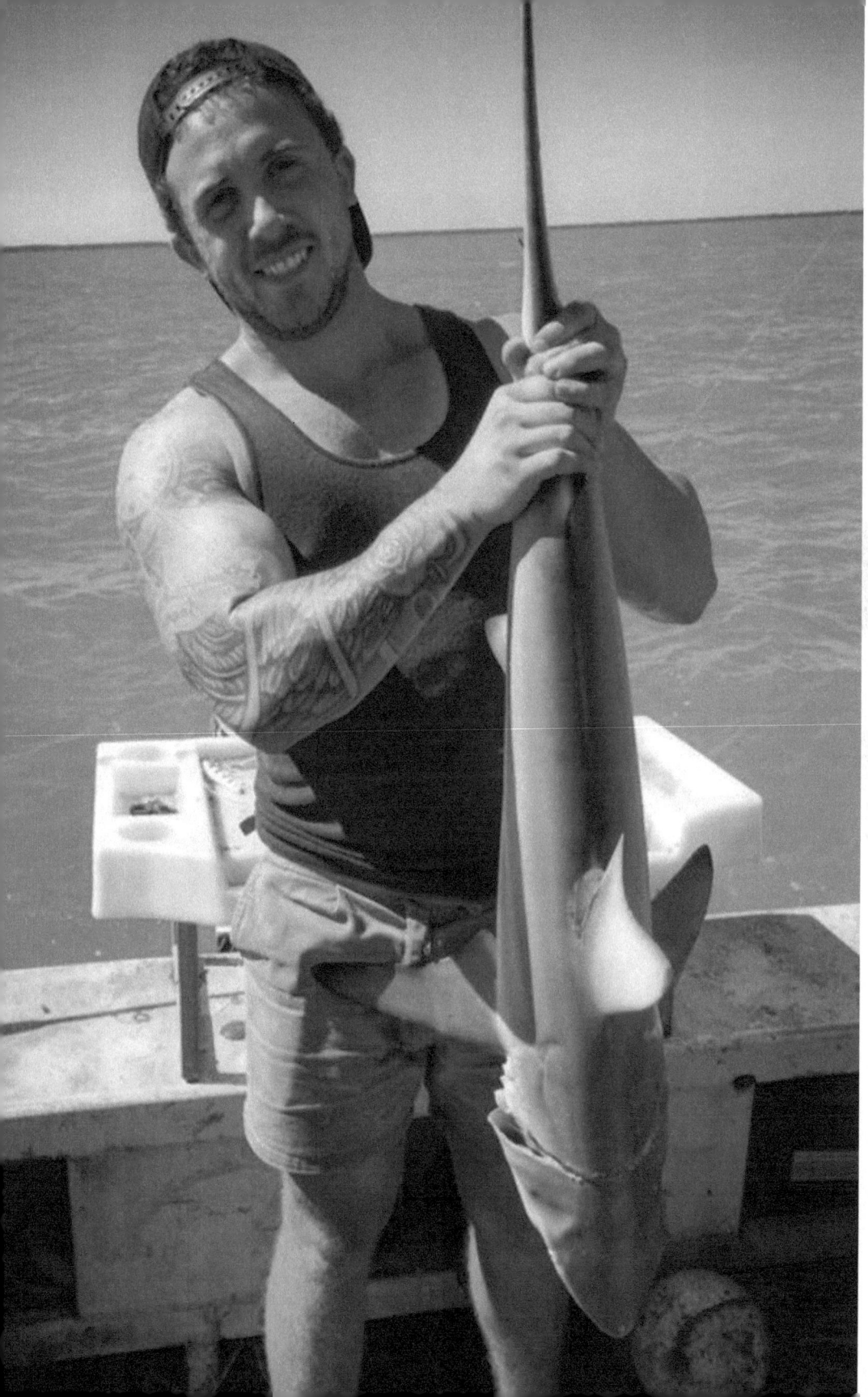

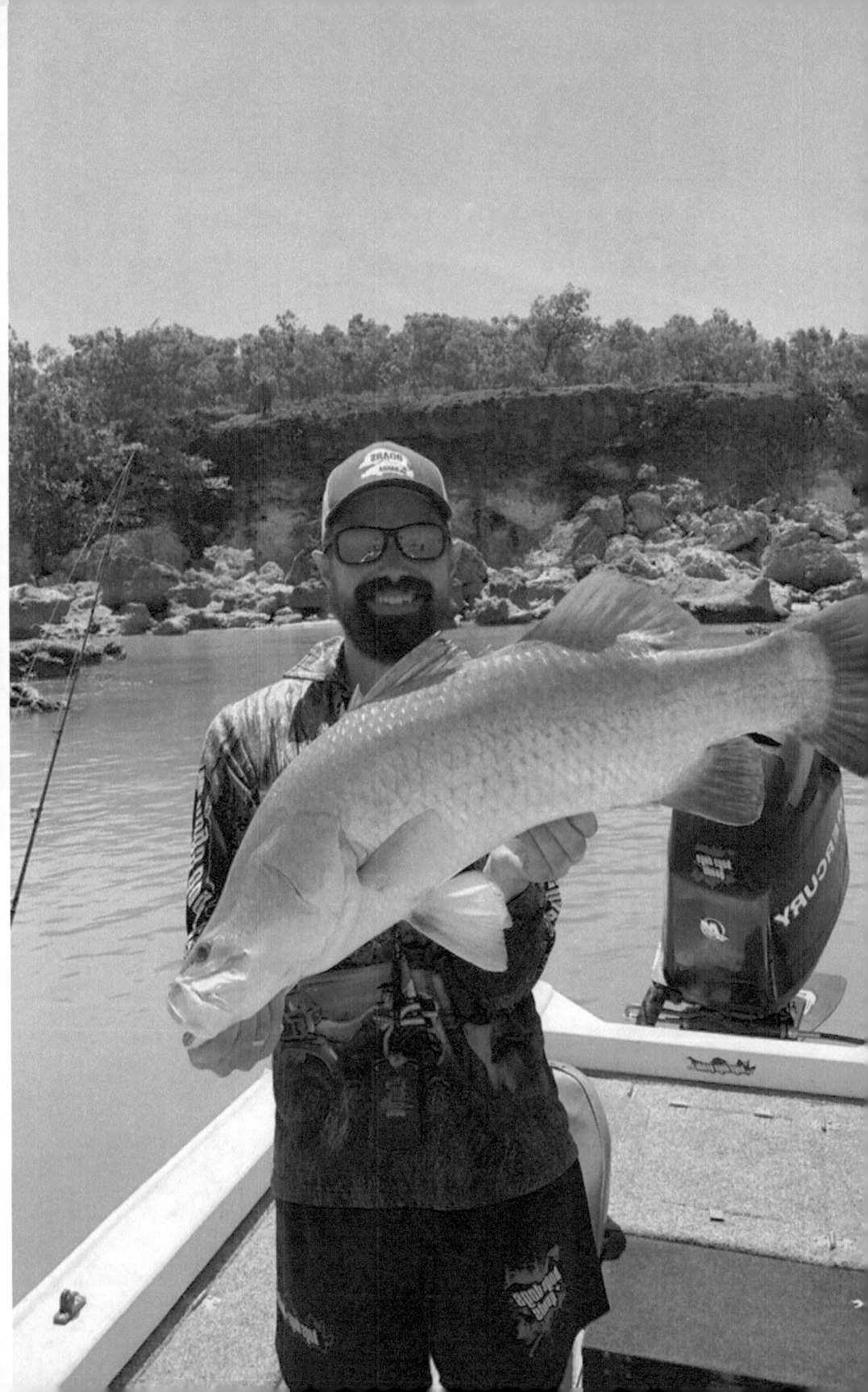

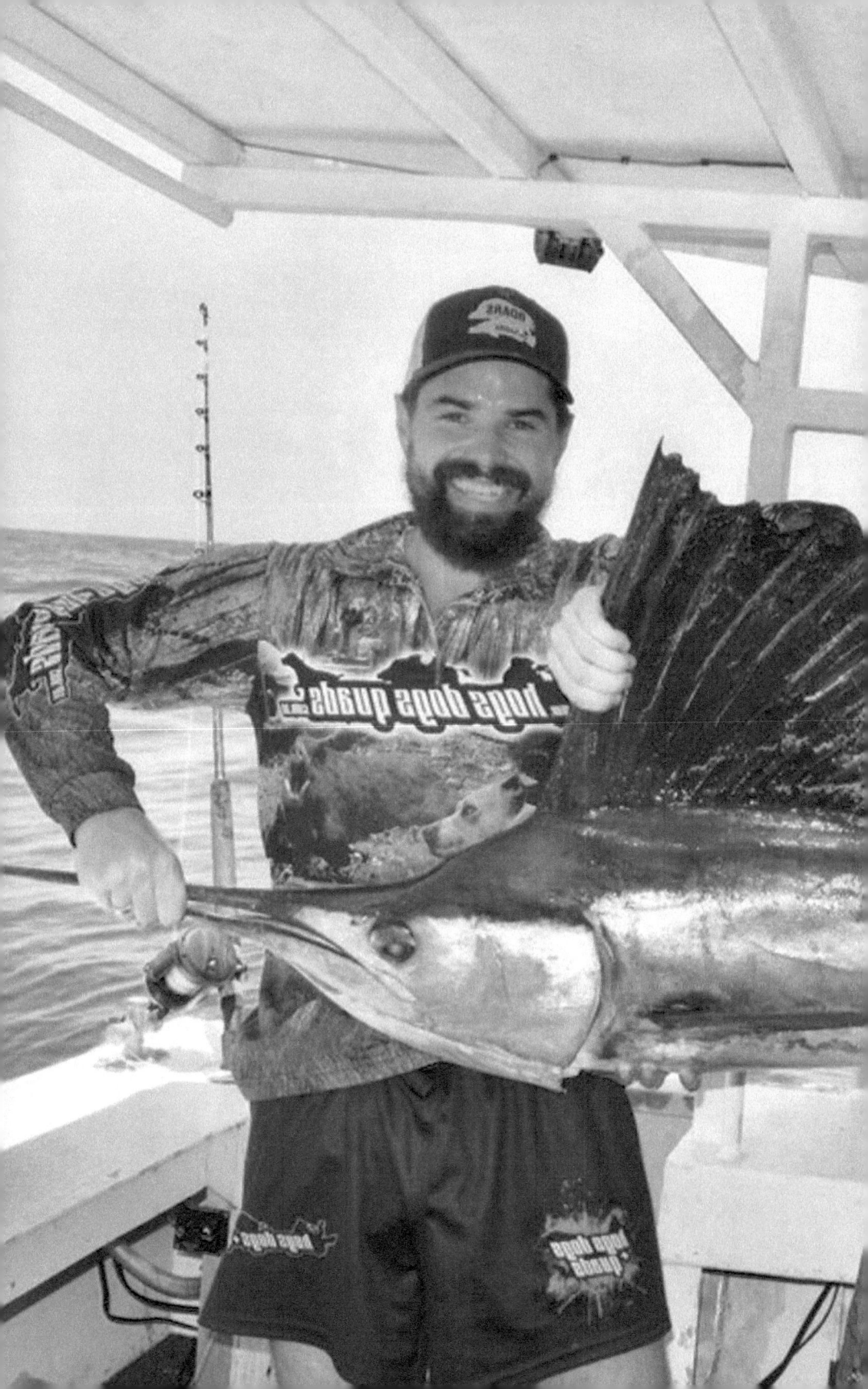

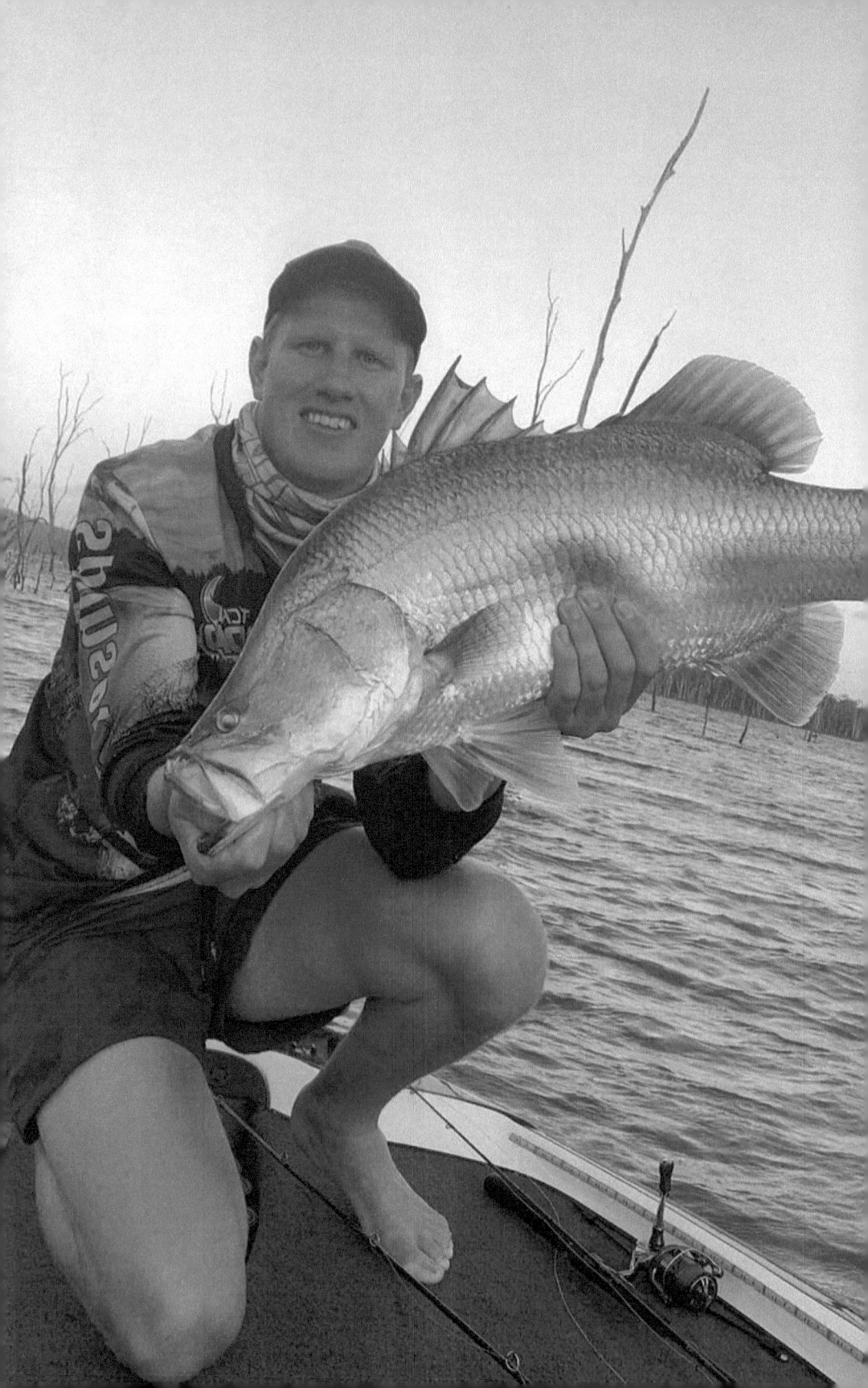

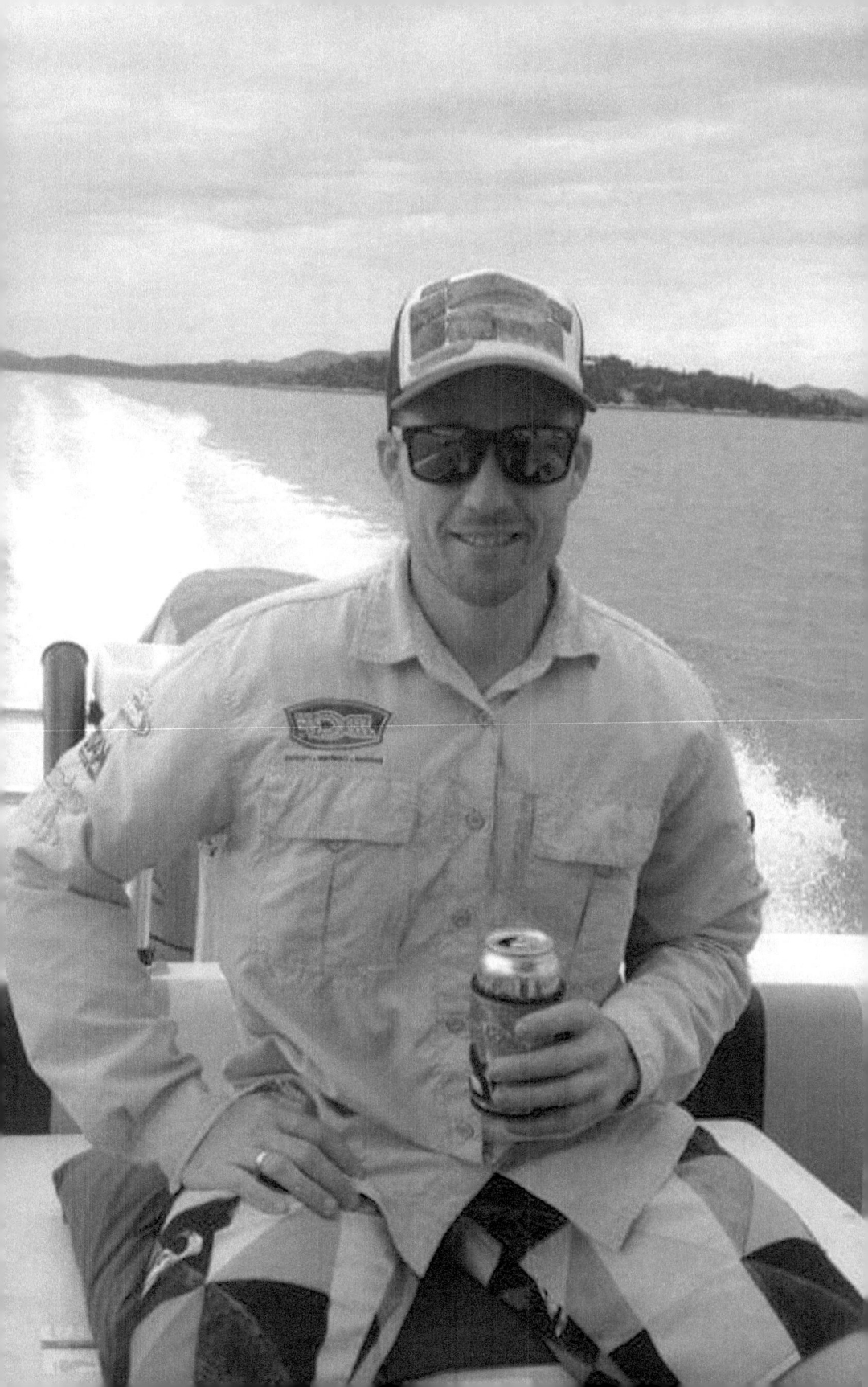

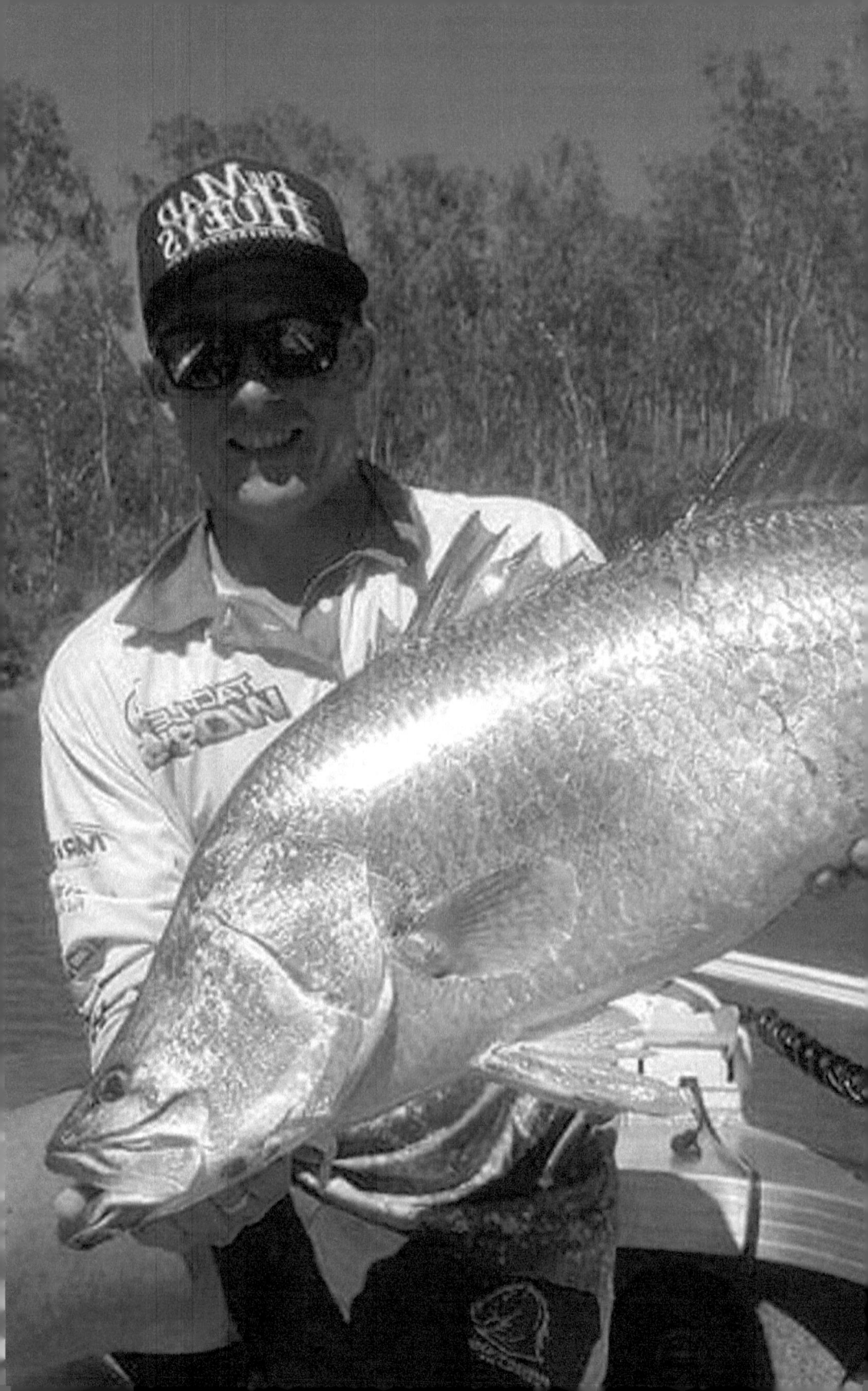

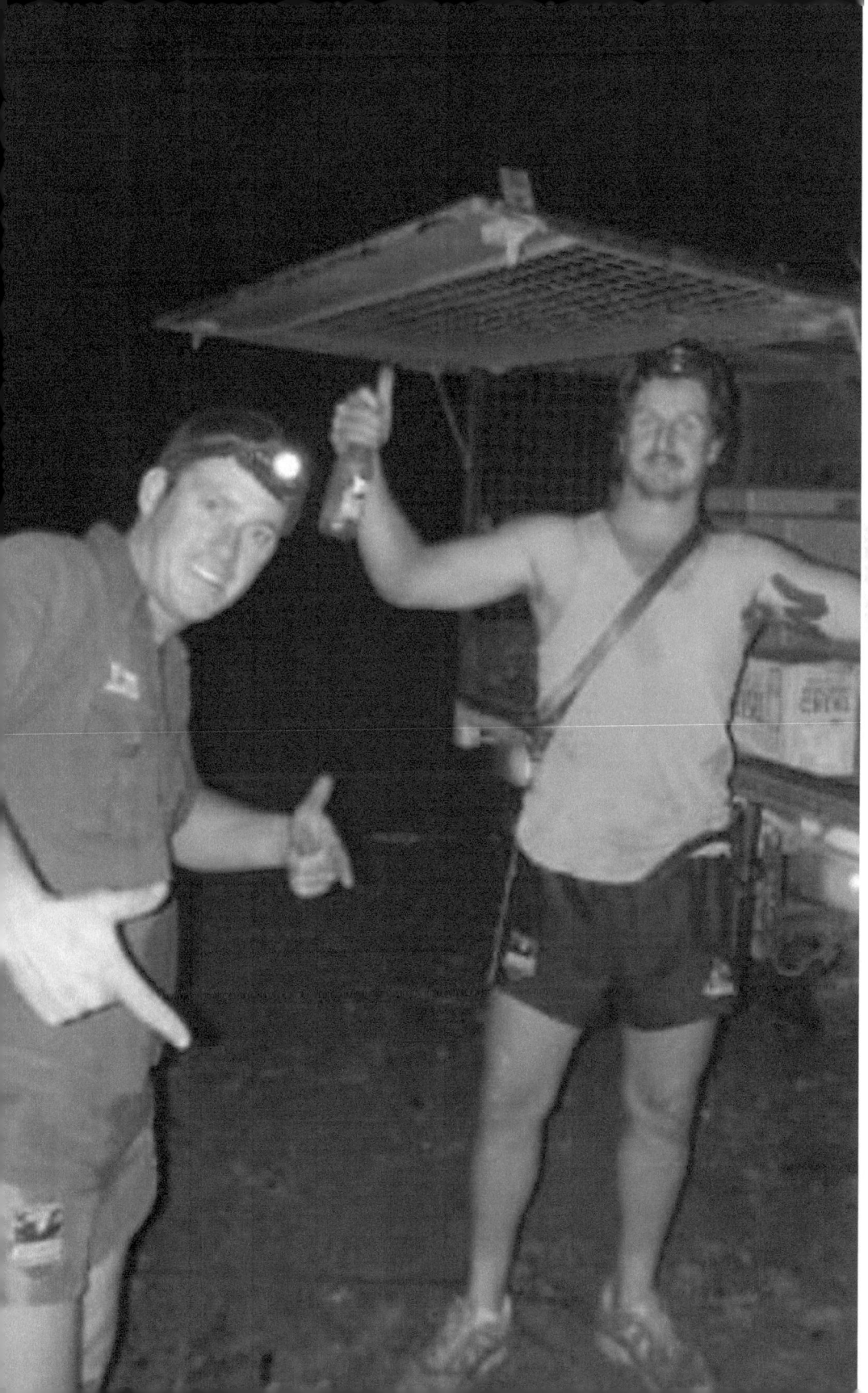

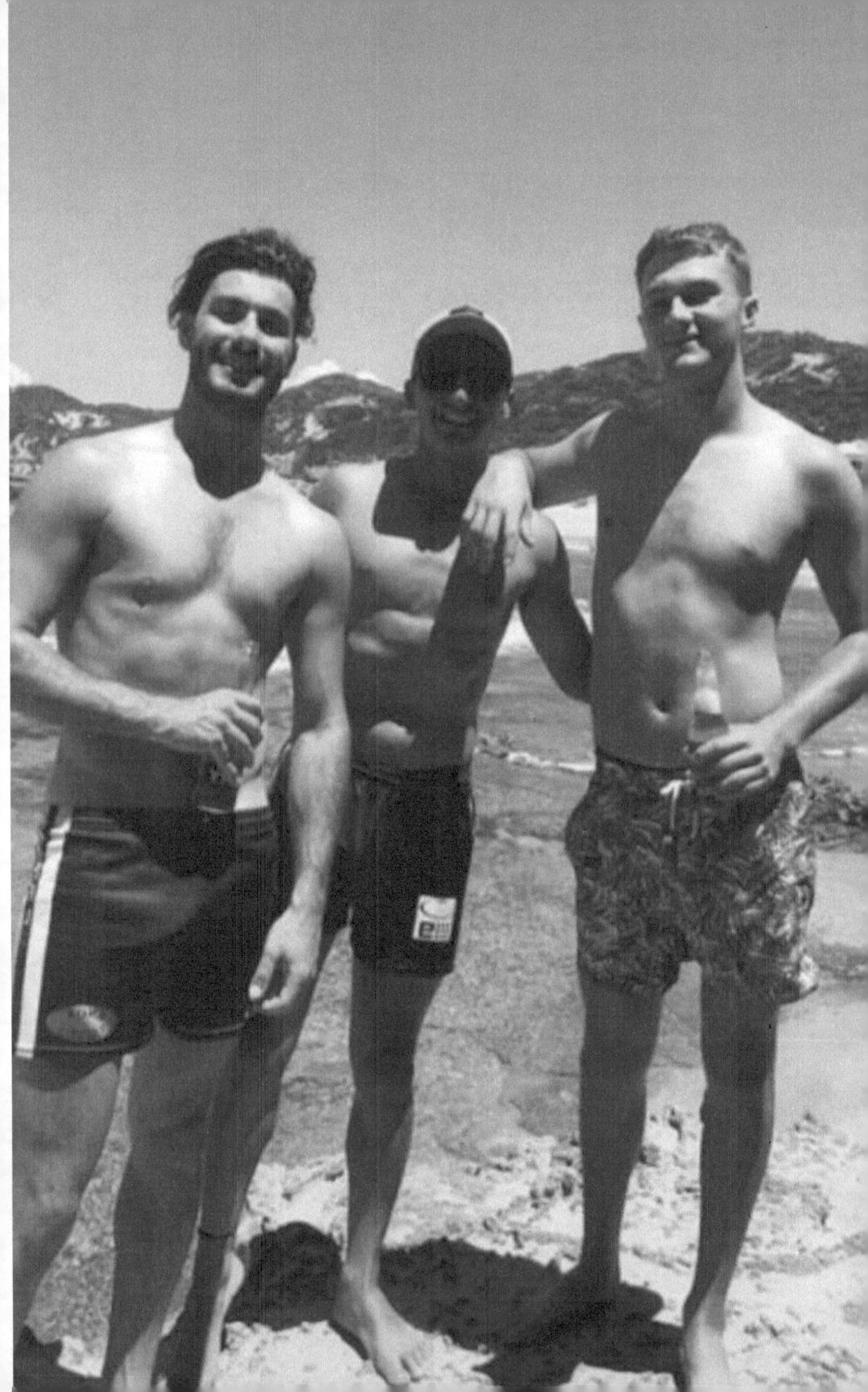

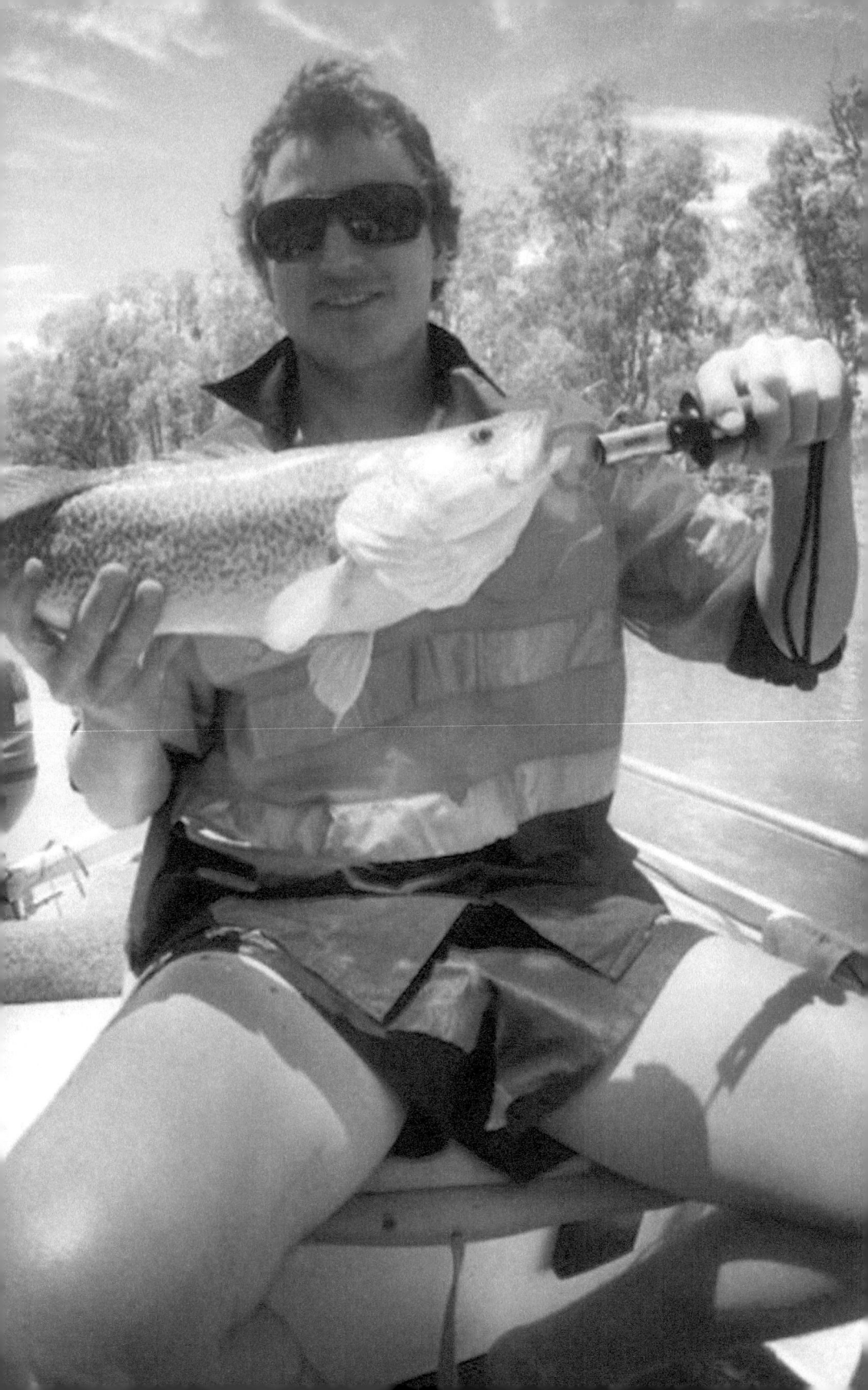

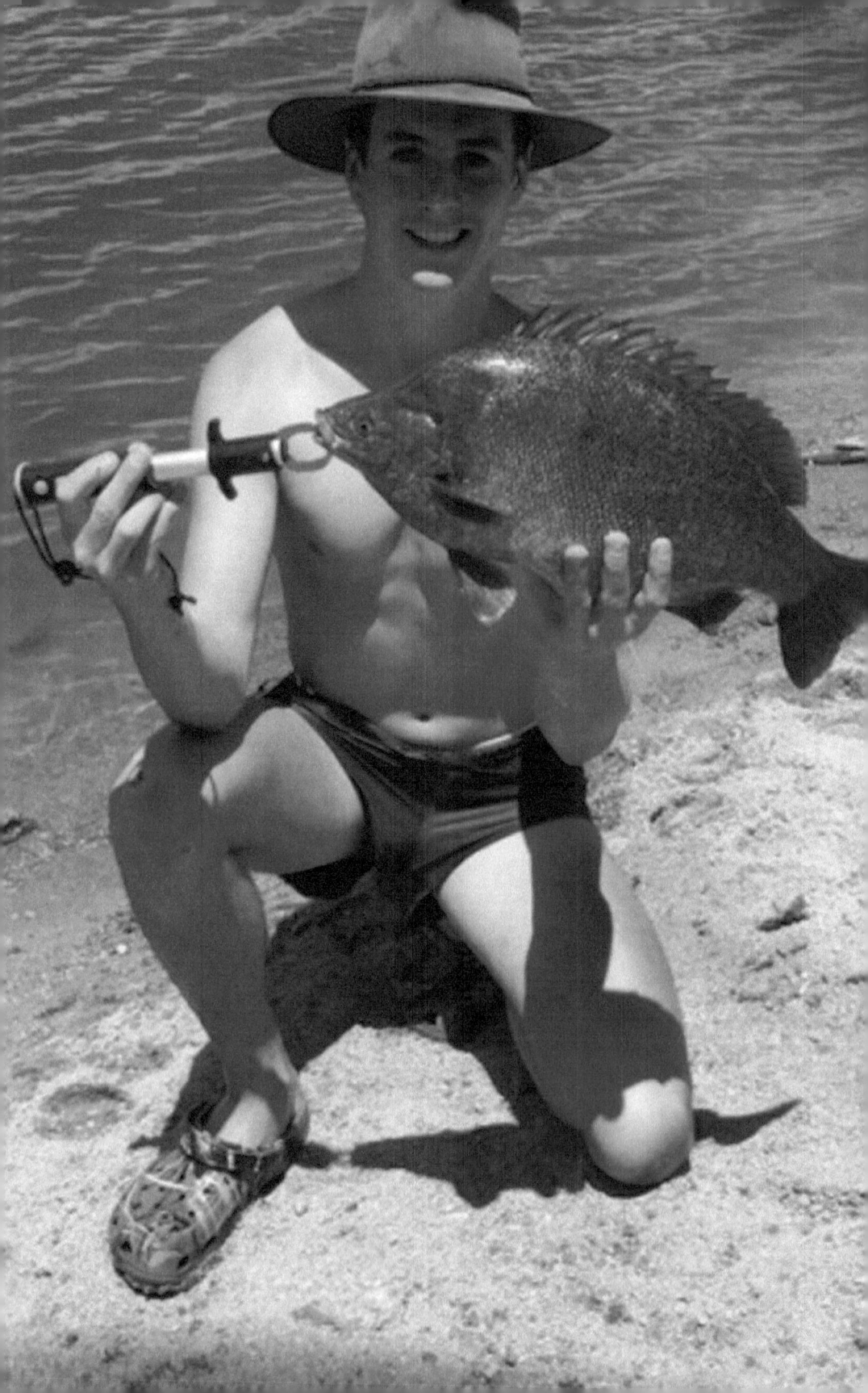

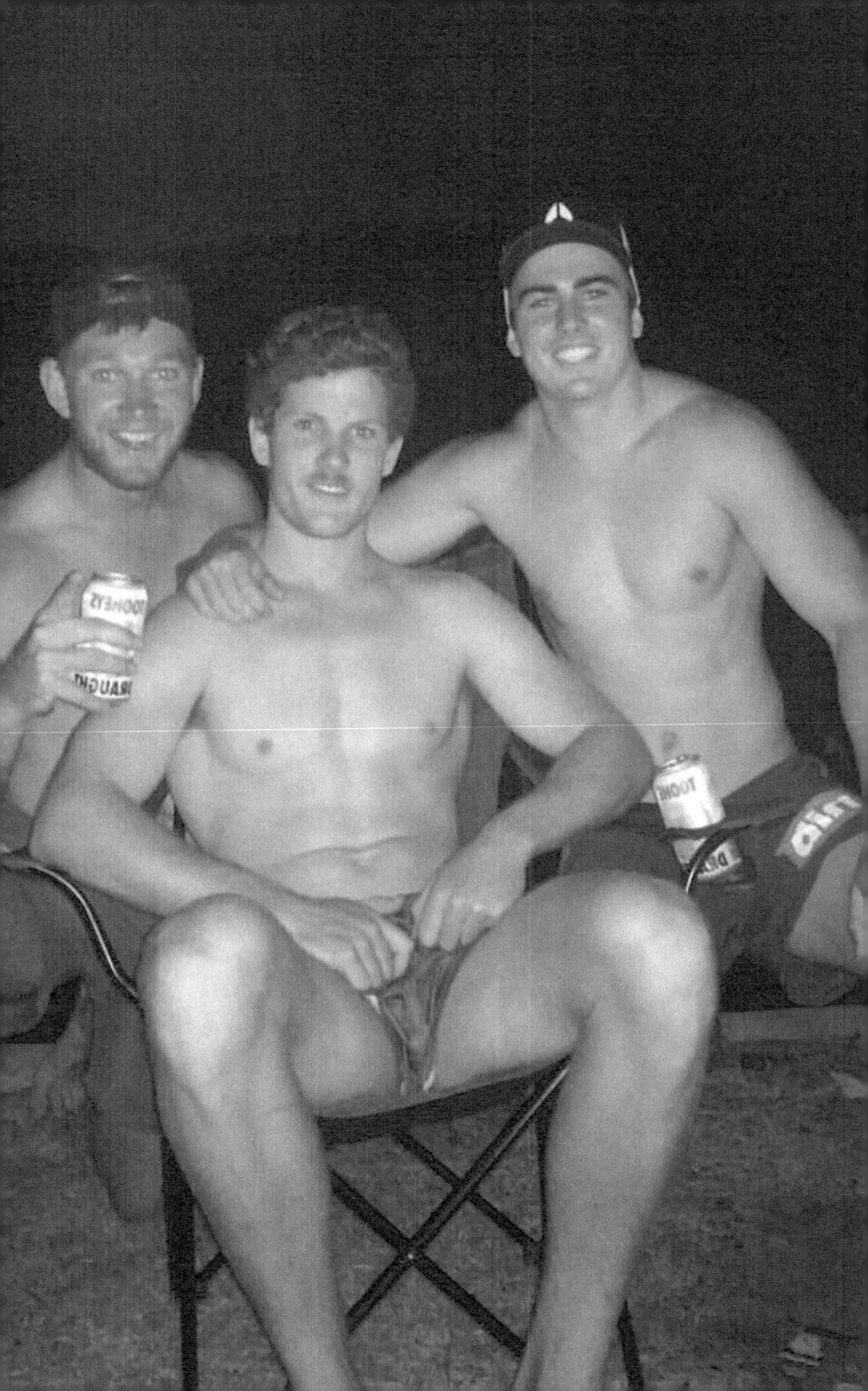

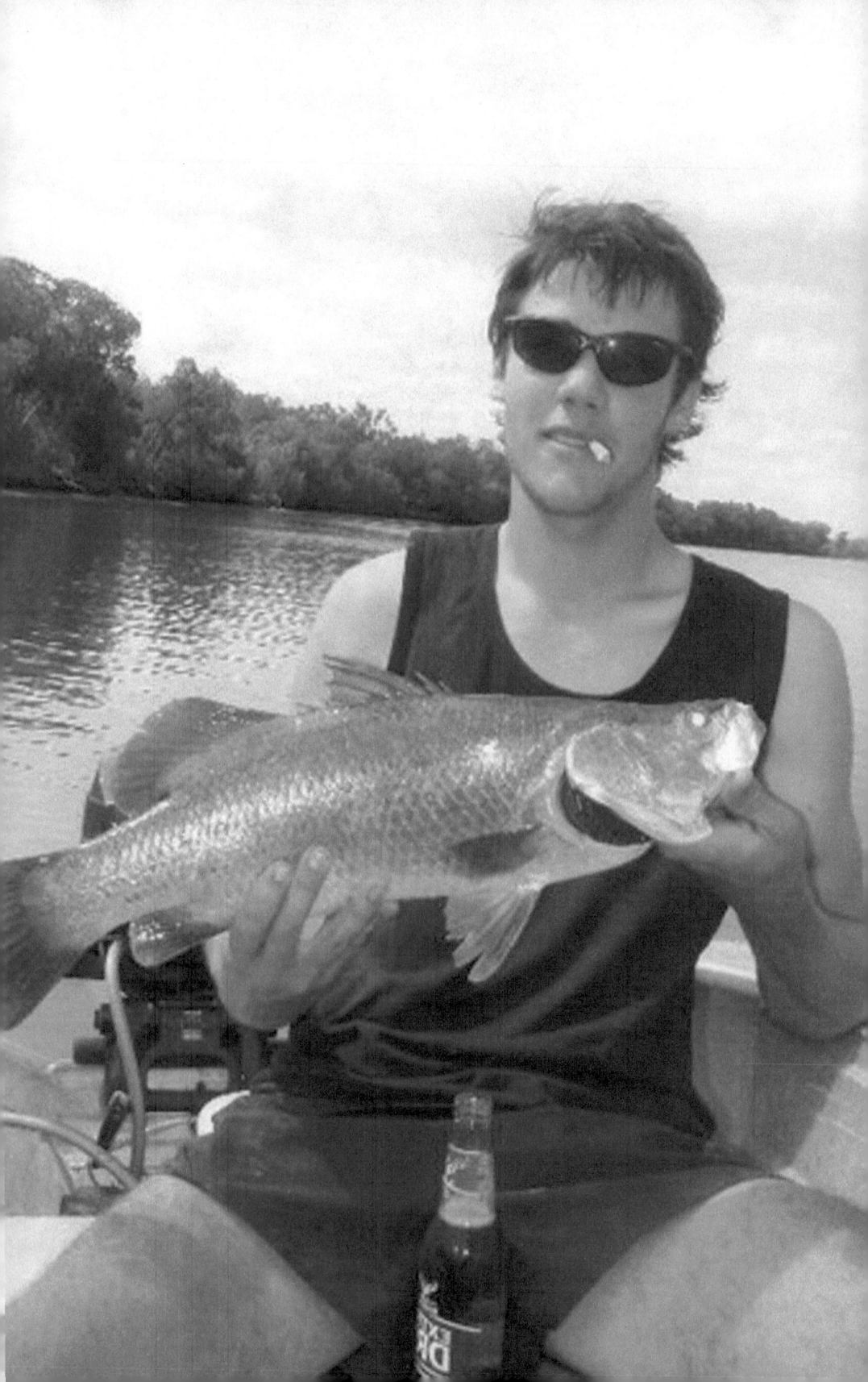

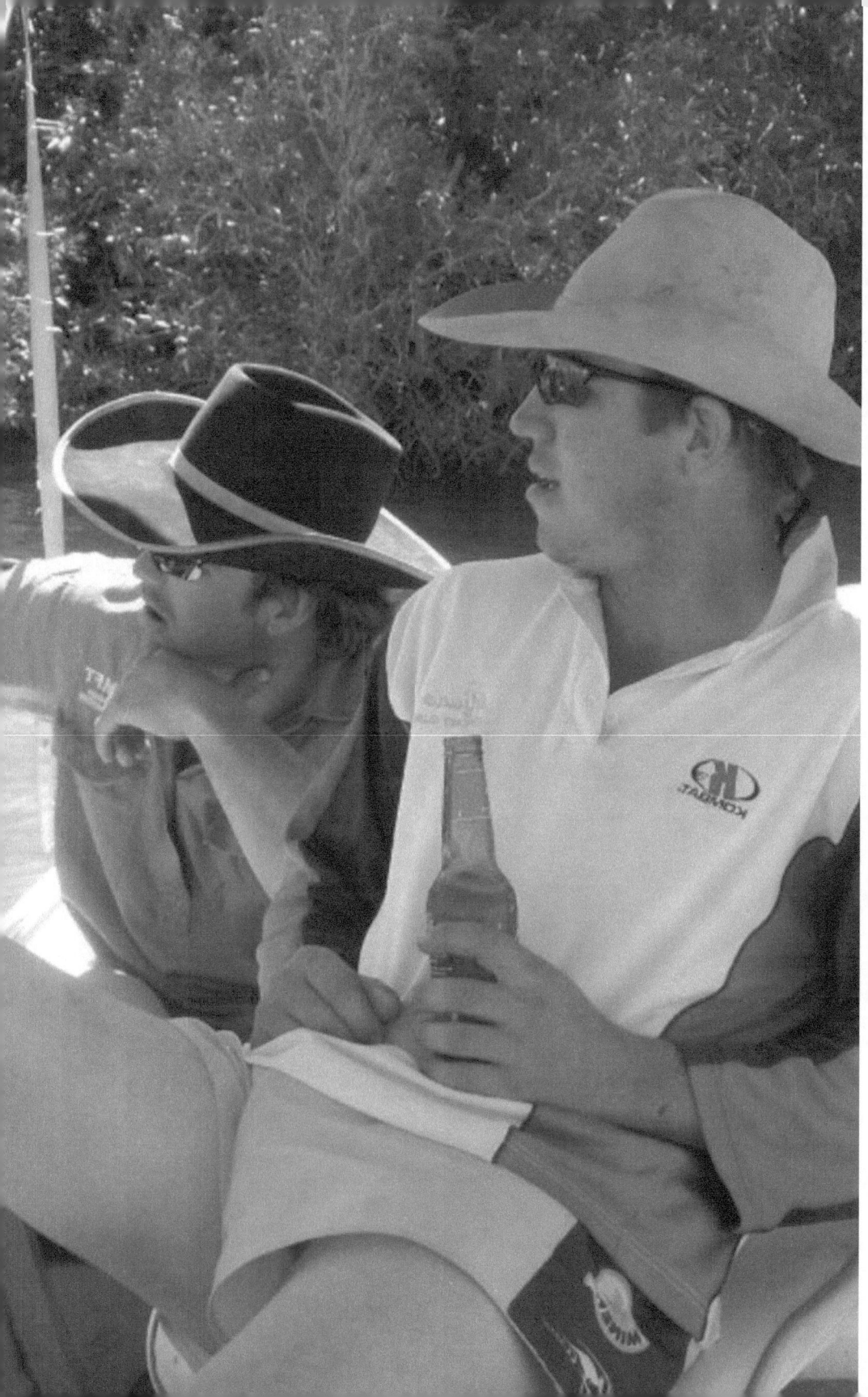

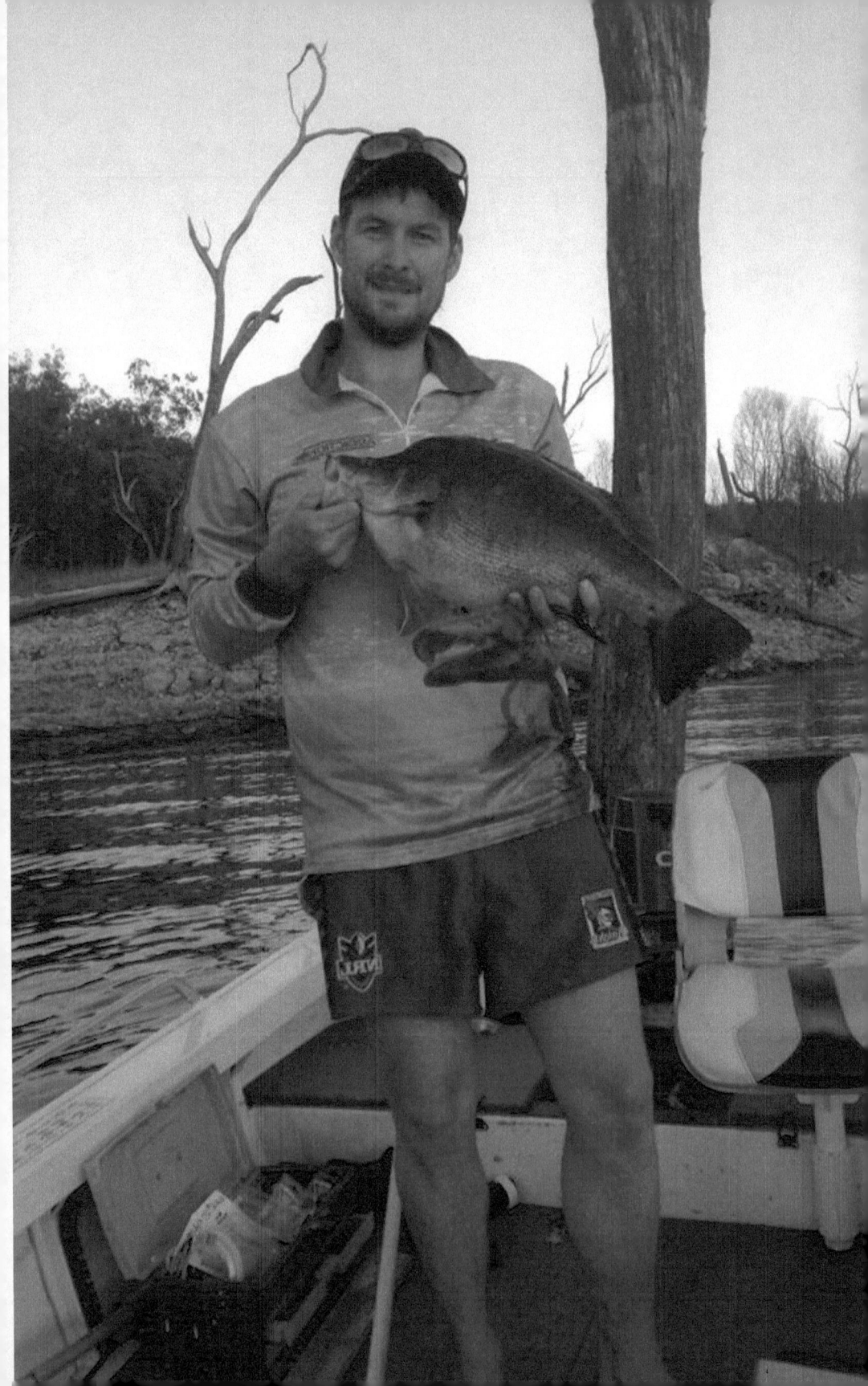

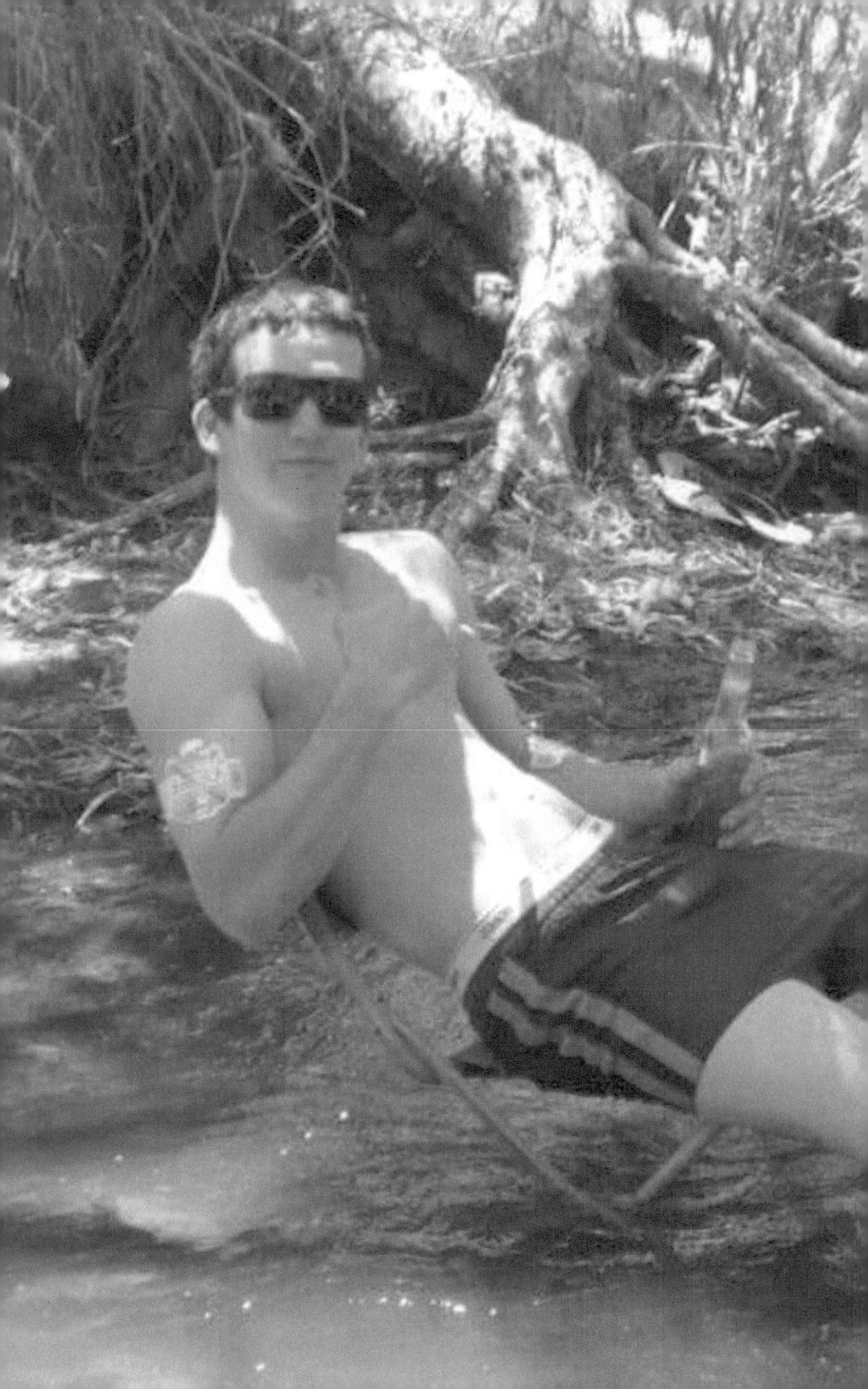

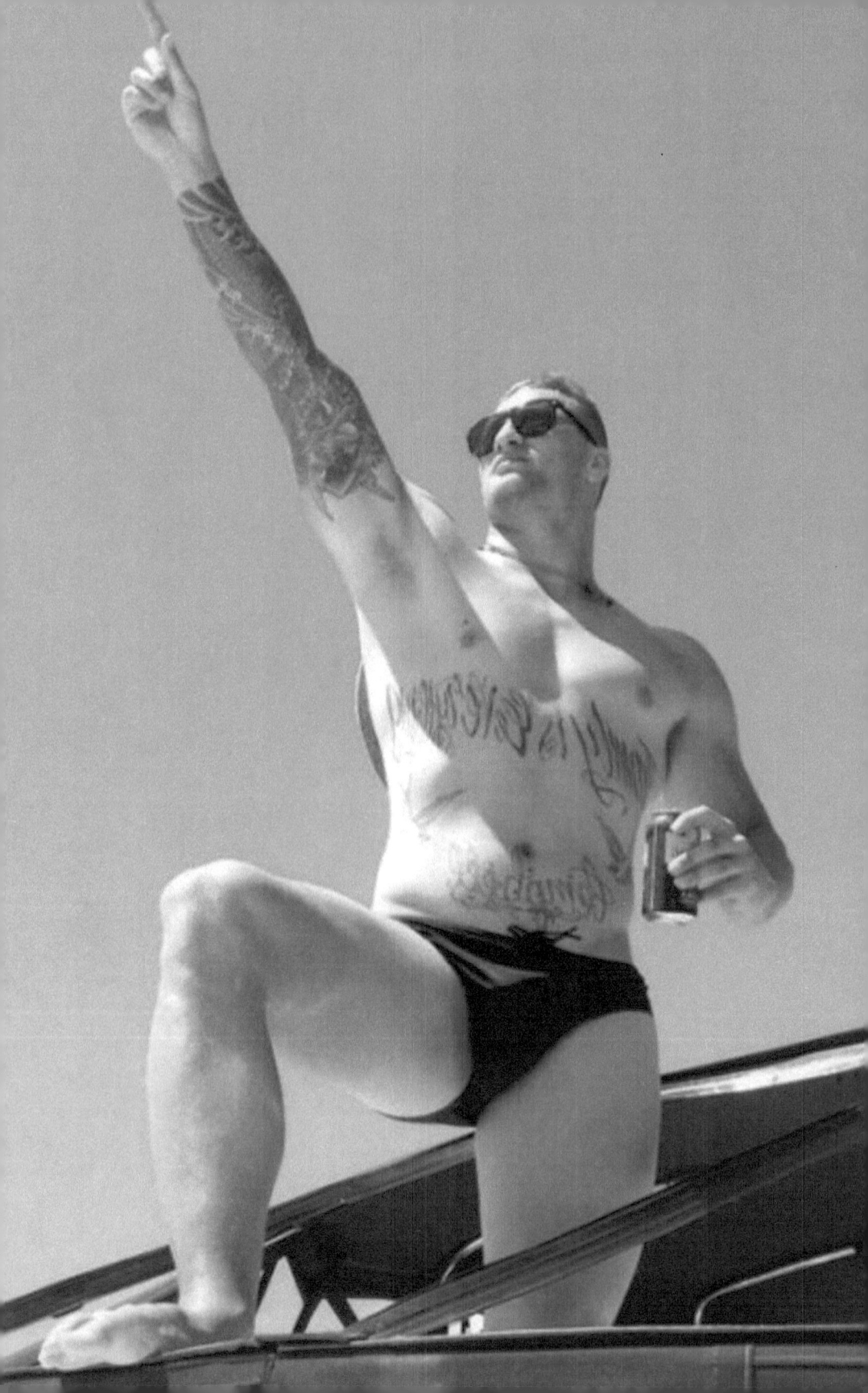

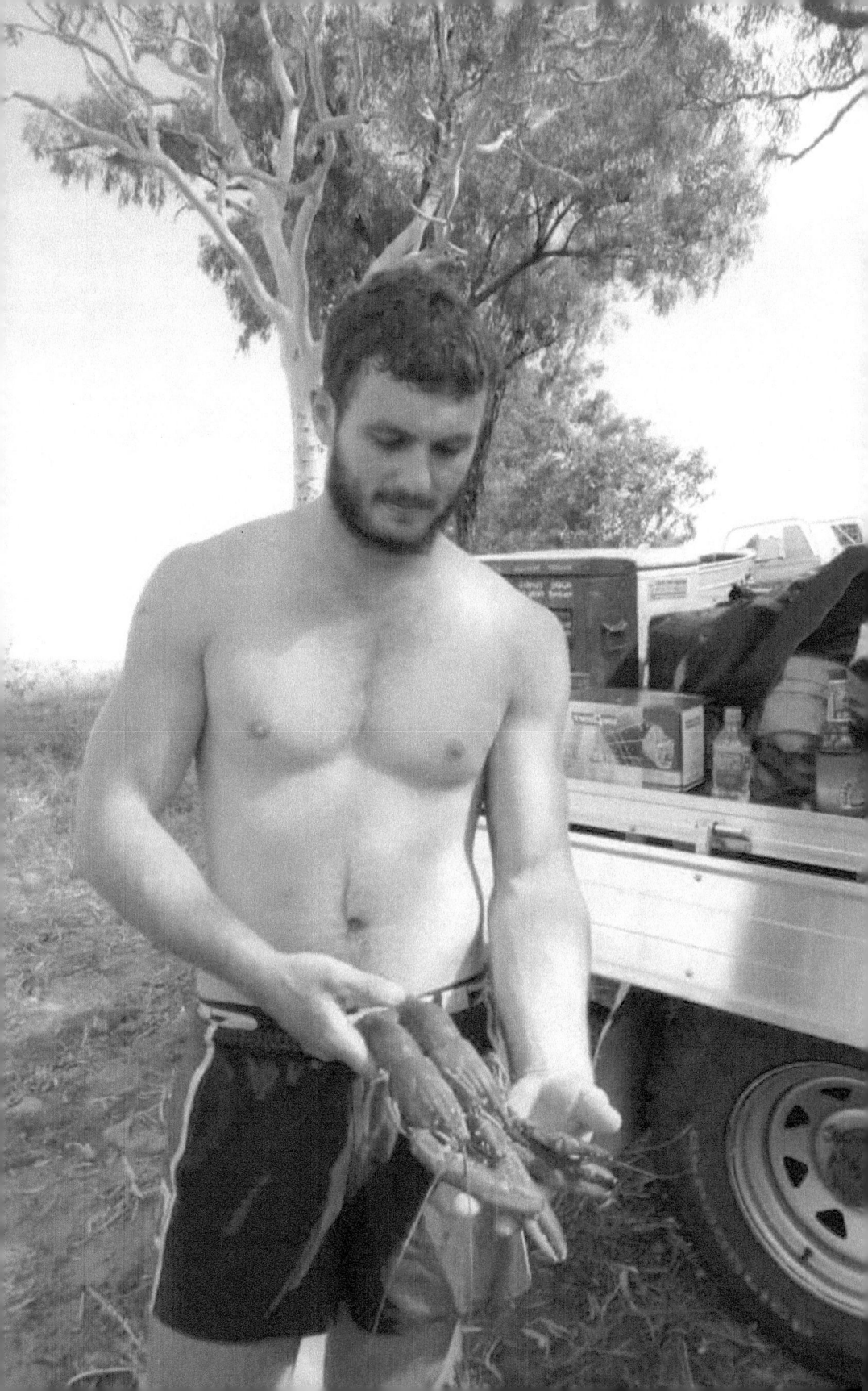

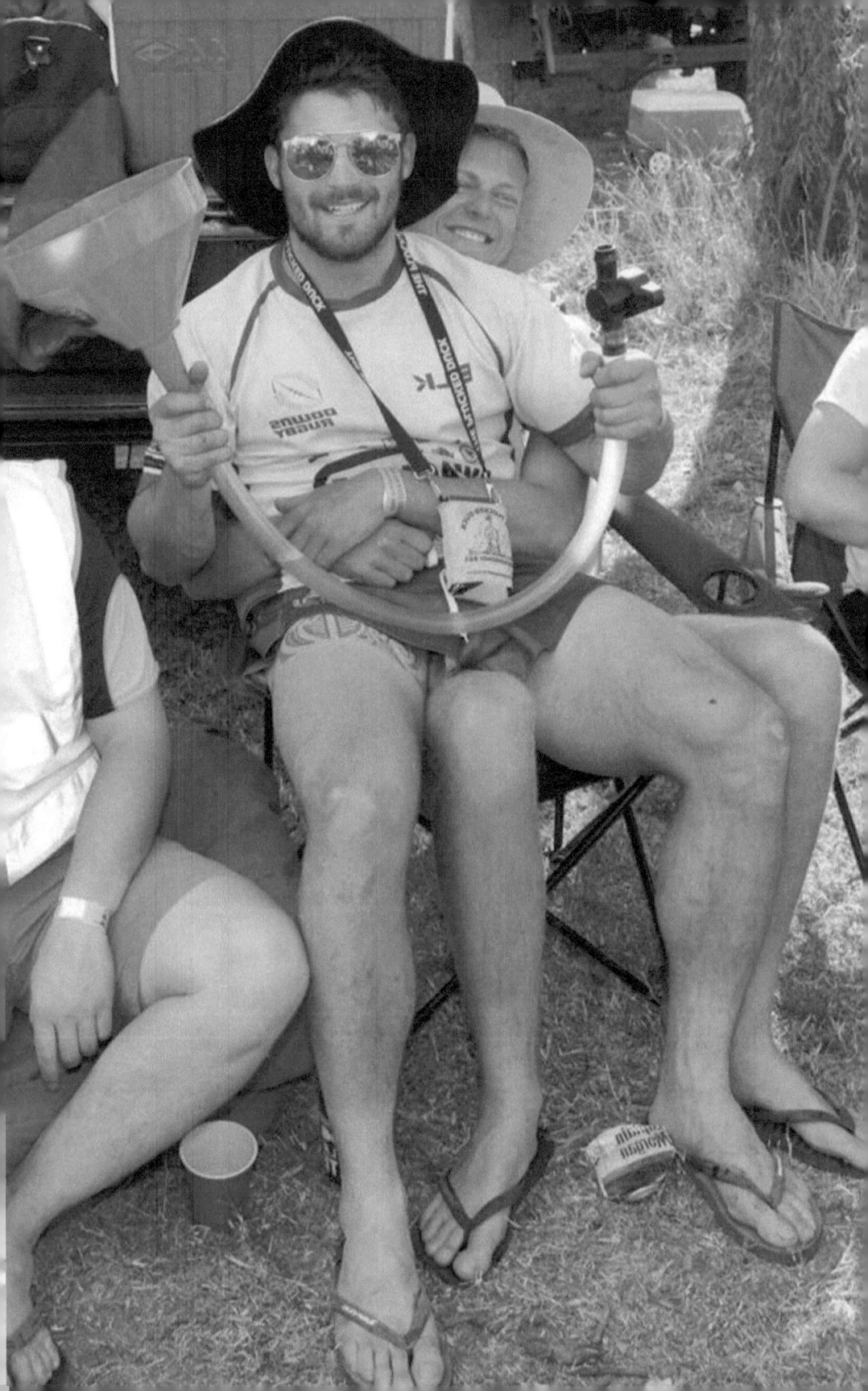

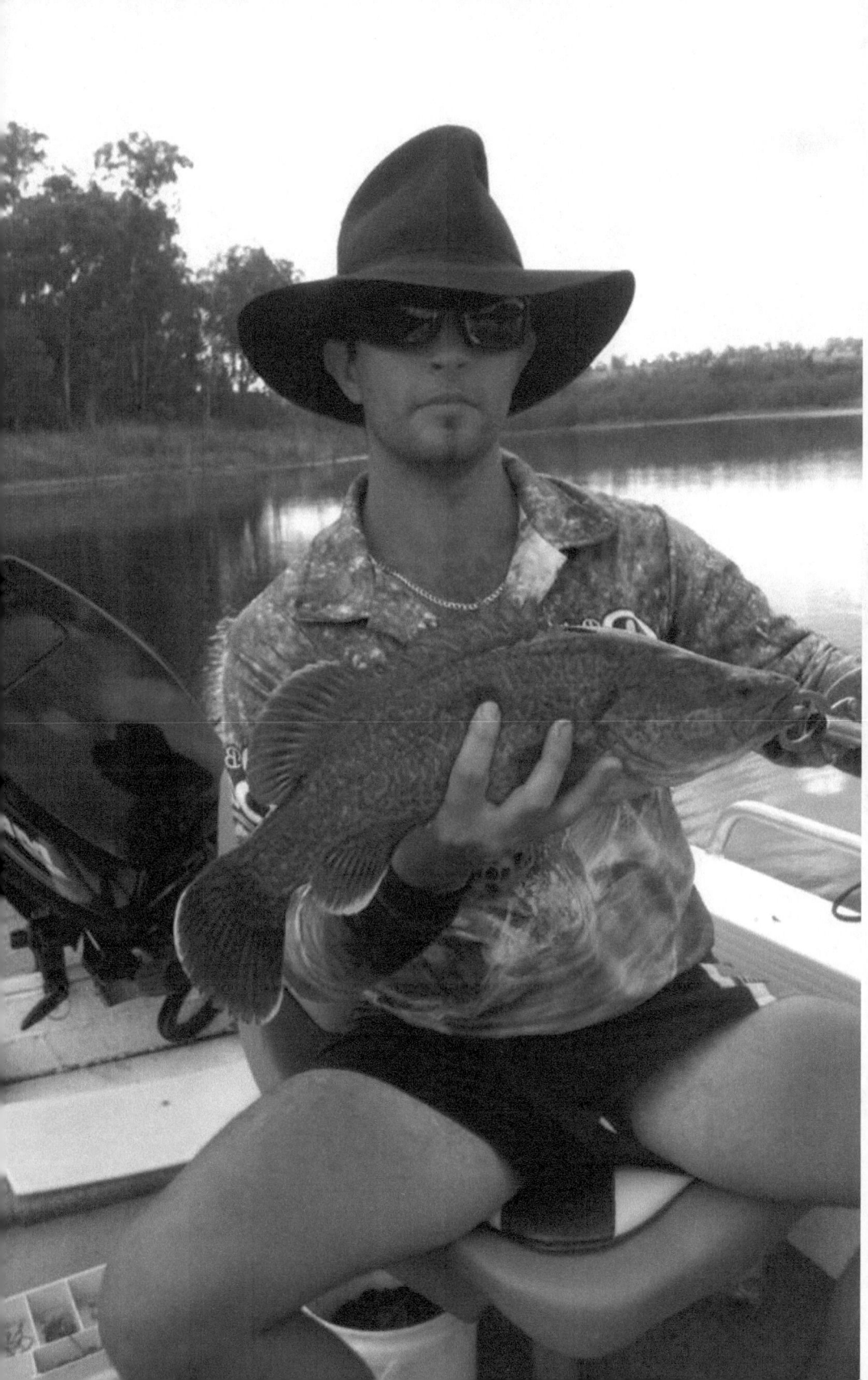

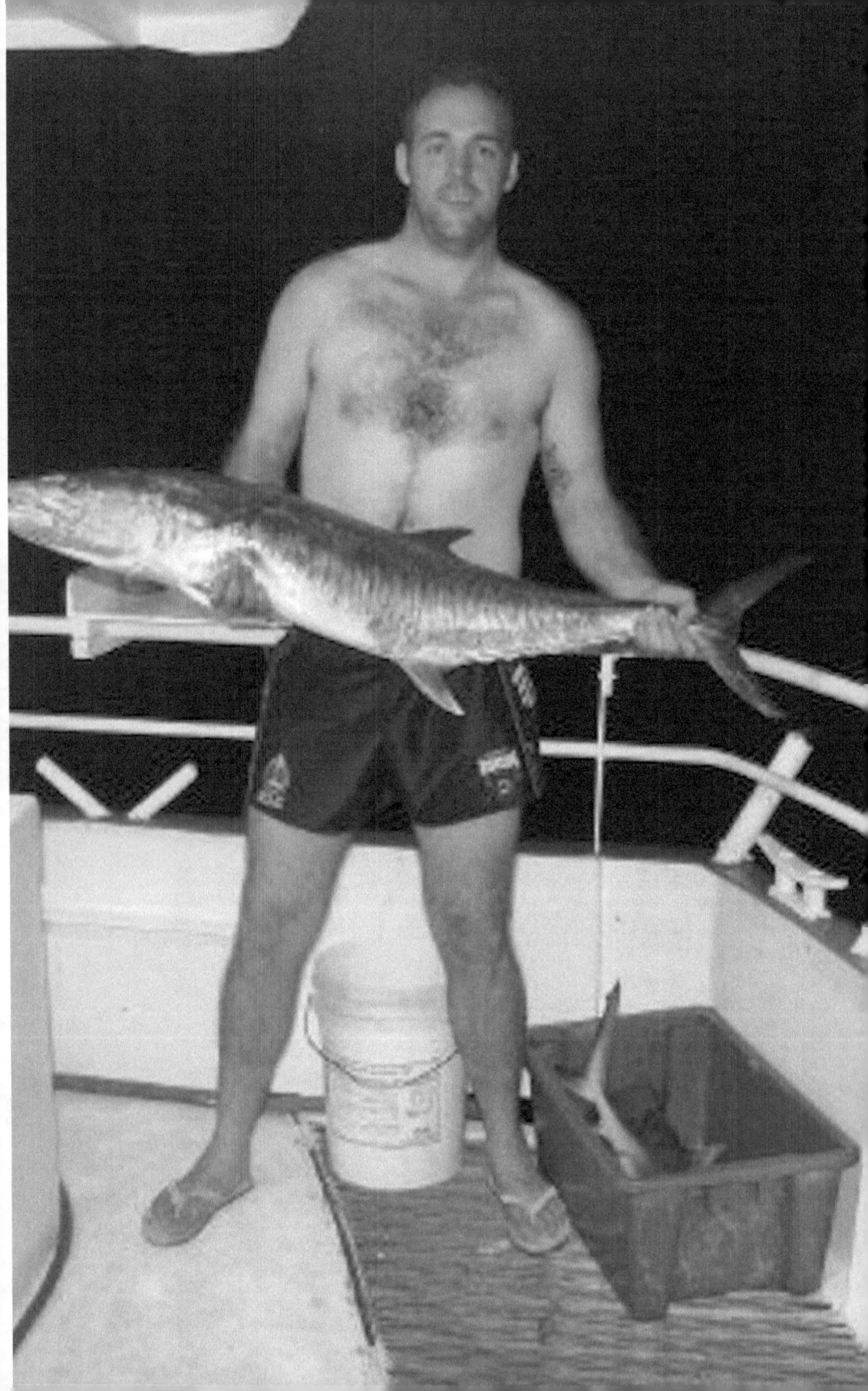

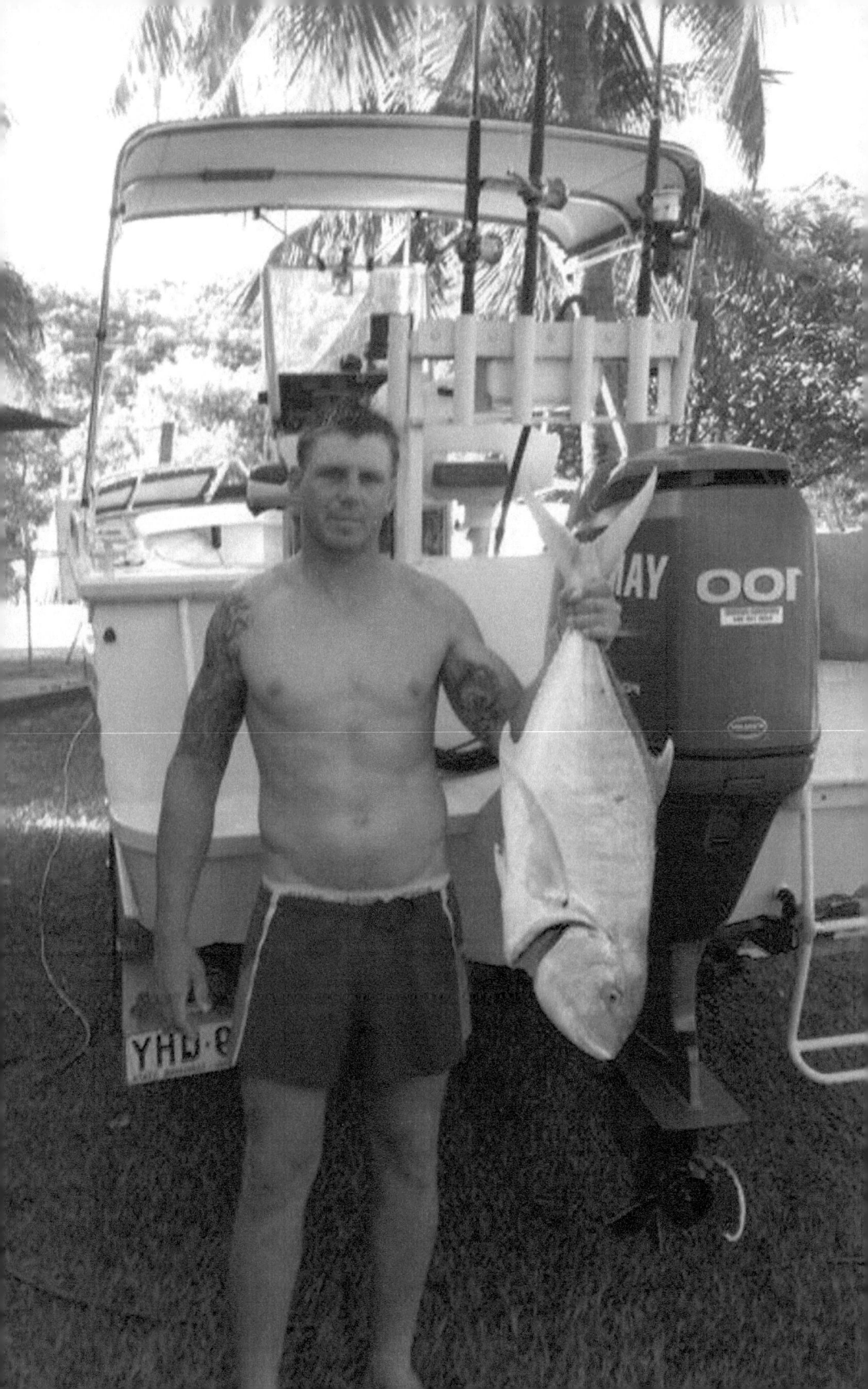

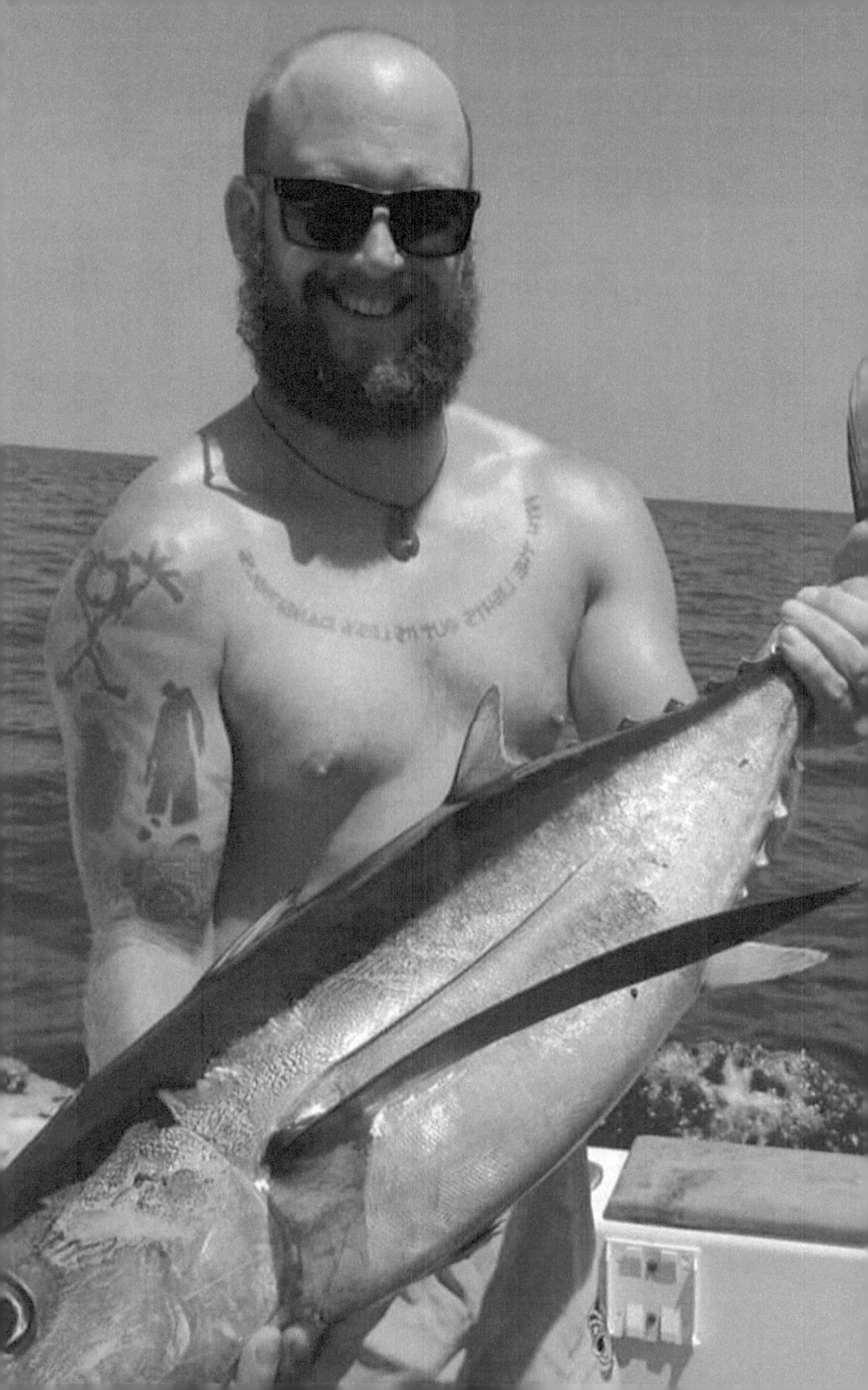

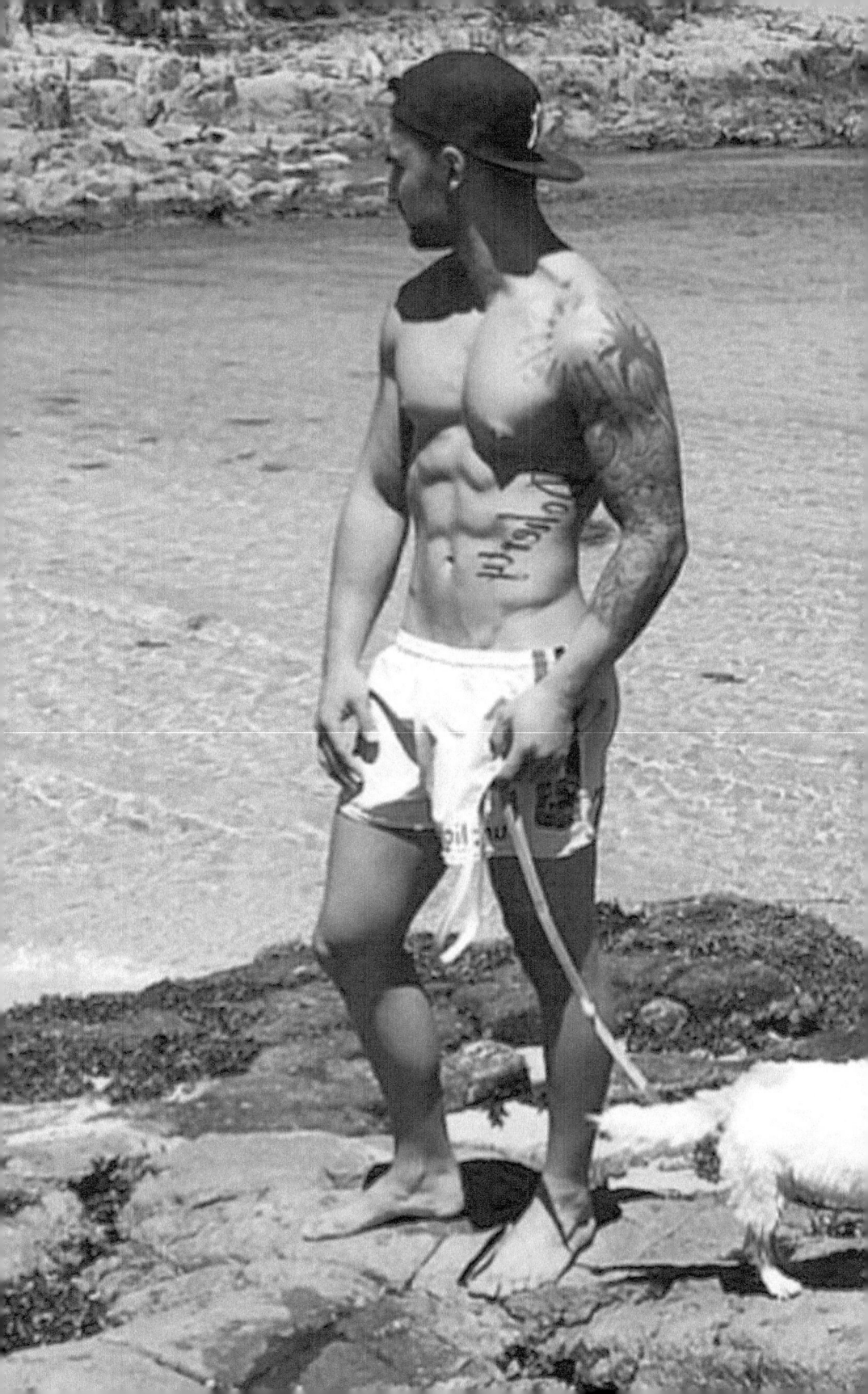

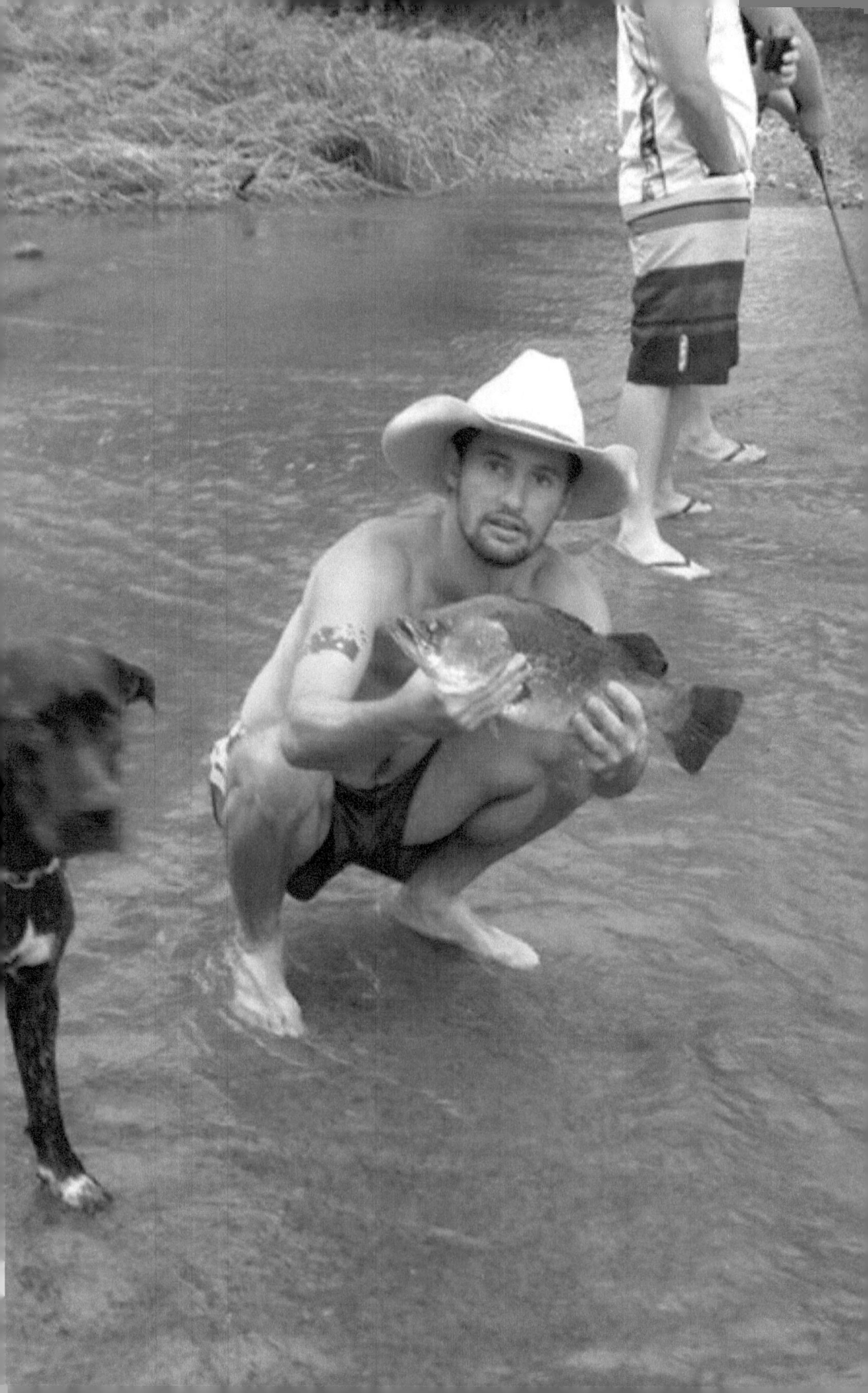

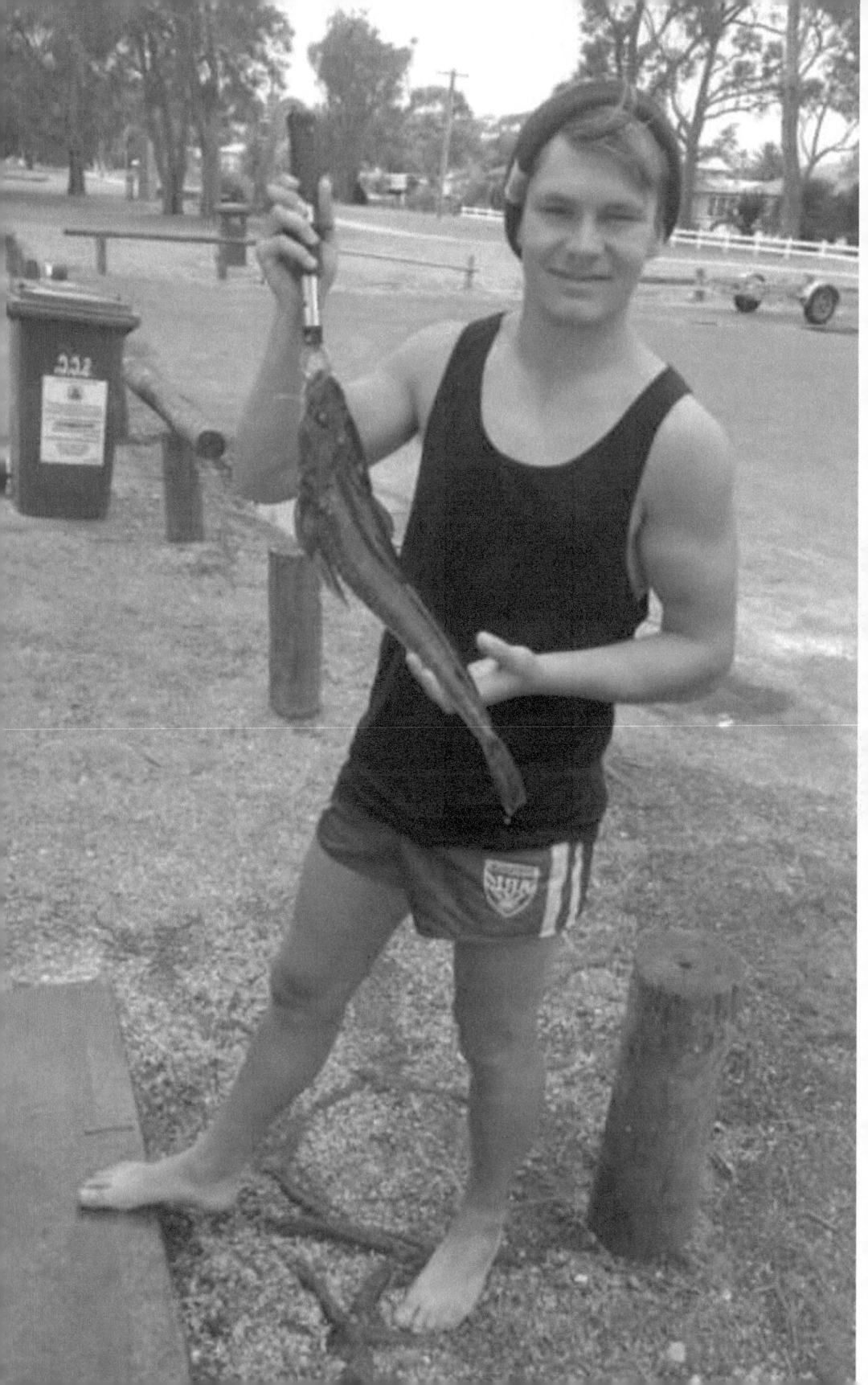

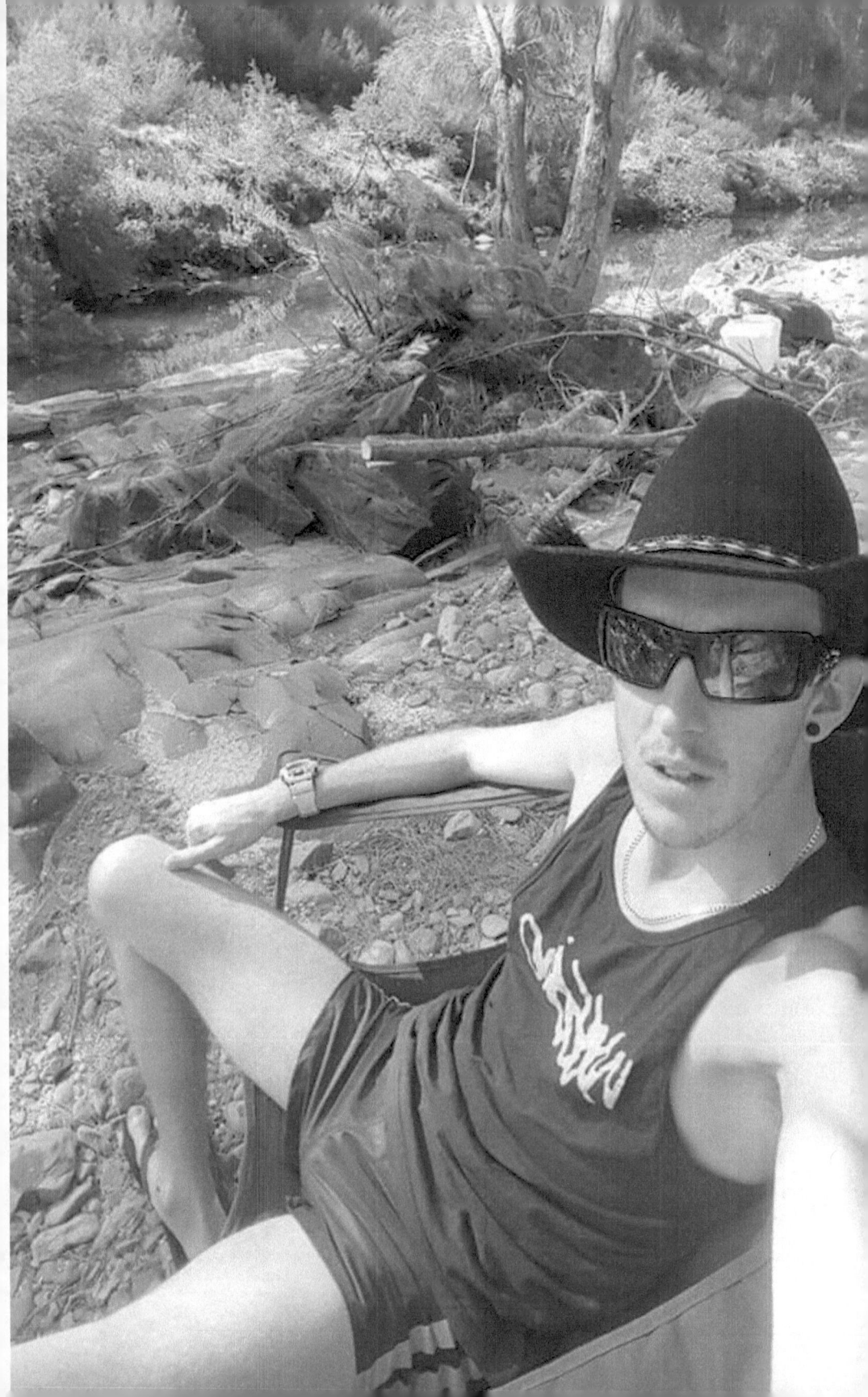